I0526981

# Dancing
# Through Covid

# Dancing
# Through Covid

ALSO BY JIM GOLD

JOURNALS

*A New Leaf: Adventures in the Creative Life*
*(Vols. 1–5)*

*A New Leaf: Adventures in the Creative Life*
*(Selected Edition)*

FICTION

*Mad Shoes: The Adventures of Sylvan Woods*

*Handfuls of Air: Stories and Poems*

*Crusader Tours*

*Carlos the Cloud and Other Stories*

CHOREOGRAPHY

*A Treasury of International Folk Dances:*
*A Step-by-Step Guide*

# Dancing Through Covid

JOURNALS 2019–2022

*Full Court Press*
*Englewood Cliffs, New Jersey*

*First Edition*

Copyright © 2022 by Jim Gold

All rights reserved.  No part of this book may be
reproduced or transmitted in any form or by any means electronic
or mechanical, including by photocopying,
by recording, or by any information storage and retrieval system,
without the express permission of the author,
except where permitted by law.

Published in the United States of America
by Full Court Press, 601 Palisade Avenue,
Englewood Cliffs, NJ 07632
*fullcourtpress.com*

ISBN 978-1-953728-04-3
Library of Congress Control No. 2022914711

*Editing and book design by Barry Sheinkopf*

FOR BERNICE

*Always*

Pandemics don't start in a vacuum. Just before they hurtle toward us, we haven't got the remotest idea they're going to transform our lives.

My journey through Covid-19 started, like yours, in just this blissful state of mind. I had two successful, smoothly functioning businesses. I loved spending time with family and friends, loved rubbing shoulders, bantering with folks in stores and on the street. I wrote zany journals and zanier fiction. I struggled for a long time to overcome my dread, as a concert-level classical guitarist, of public recitals. I tried to shed light as well on my fascination with the stock market, on my hungers and loves and illuminations. I had published over a dozen volumes of journals, short stories, and book-length fiction, and I was looking forward to publishing more. I reveled in folk dance, folk tours, and published a treasury of my dance choreographies, too.

To say that I took all of that for granted is true enough, I suppose, but it fails to suggest what I felt at the time. Like almost everybody I have spoken to about the years before Covid, it was everything I knew—filled with familiar ups and downs, triumphs and disasters, and the same old me.

That everything has in some important respects been swept away as *Dancing With Covid* comes to press. I thought it important to allow its voice to be heard here as well, which is why the book opens long before the pandemic began. Maybe one of these days we'll all get back to that time. And maybe not.

—J.G.,
Teaneck, 2022

# Table of Contents

## AUTHOR'S NOTE

Pandemics don't start in a vacuum. Just before they hurtle toward us, we haven't got the remotest idea they're going to transform our lives.

My journey through Covid-19 started, like yours, in just this blissful state of mind. I had two successful, smoothly functioning businesses. I loved spending time with family and friends, loved rubbing shoulders, bantering with folks in stores and on the street. I wrote zany journals and zanier fiction. I struggled for a long time to overcome my dread, as a concert-level classical guitarist, of public recitals. I tried to shed light as well on my fascination with the stock market, on my hungers and loves and illuminations. I had published over a dozen volumes of journals, short stories, and book-length fiction, and I was looking forward to publishing more. I reveled in folk dance, folk tours, and published a treasury of my dance choreographies, too.

To say that I took all of that for granted is true enough, I suppose, but it fails to suggest what I felt at the time. Like almost everybody I have spoken to about the years before Covid, it was everything I knew—filled with familiar ups and downs, triumphs and disasters, and the same old me.

That everything has in some important respects been swept away as *Dancing With Covid* comes to press. I thought it important to allow its voice to be heard here as well, which is why the book opens long before the pandemic began. Maybe one of these days we'll all get back to that time. And maybe not.

—J.G.,
Teaneck, 2022

# Table of Contents

## LAND OF SUCCESS

## RETURN

# Stepping Out

# Enjoyment

*Friday, July 5, 2019*
*The Castle Has a New Master*

I used to see improvement and enjoyment as part of each other, as twins, as two sides of the same coin. The process of self-improvement was enjoyable, and I enjoyed improving.

However, today I'm wondering about that division.

Self-improvement is part of the journey to get there. But enjoyment is the end of the road. It occurs, happens, is felt, when you are there.

Seen in this way, the two are quite separate, different mental states.

Now my aim is for enjoyment. If I improve along the way, that's fine. If I don't, that's fine, too. In this scheme, improvement is beside the point.

*Sunday, July 7, 2019*
*Nes Gadol: A Miracle*

Today another miraculous new beginning. For the first time in 40 or 50 years, perhaps even the first time ever, this morning I began my guitar playing, not with legato or scale warms-ups, or even a classical guitar piece warm-up, but instead dove right into singing "Dark As a Dungeon."

I'd never started guitar practice with a song and, of course, in my old concert life, I never did either. I always needed to "prove myself" by starting with a classical guitar piece. Then, once I showed the audience I could actually "do something," was sophisticated, worthy, not just "another folk singer" but could play something classical, once I proved I was okay, then I could relax, lie back, do easy stuff like folk singing, humor, stories, and especially lead group singing (which was a real gas, a riot of fun), and have a great time.

But evidently, I've somehow freed myself with my new focus on enjoyment—or, rather, on how to enjoy what I'm doing.

This morning I followed "Dungeon" with "Blues My Naughty Sweetie Gave To Me," focusing on diction.

Then, to my amazement, I dropped down to playing Bach's "Gavotte in D," followed by his "Gavotte en Rondeau." And it felt loose, easy, comfortable, and fine. I was totally at ease with my "audience," although of course there was no audience, only the one in my imagination. But those imaginary people were part of the family.

Then I sang a few bars of "This Little Light of Mine."

Then I played "Alhambra" slow, easy, comfortable. No problem. The "audience" just sat there accepting it, loving every sensual stroke I plucked on each string—and especially enjoying the pleasure in my index finger as it plucked along in friendly, fun, joy-filled fashion.

As Moses said, "This is my first exodus. I've never done one before." It has never happened in my lifetime. I'm at a new place. It's a miracle, a nes gadol. Even my mother would like it.

### Tuesday, July 16, 2019
### Successful Suffering: Push to the Limit

Got up 4:30 a.m. Nice.

Strangely, believing I want, need, even like suffering is a good way to think. It helps me face painful situations. And of these, in life, there are many. Instead of feeling like a failure because I am not "enjoying" my tours, or exercises, or whatever I'm doing, I now feel things are right and in place because I am appropriately suffering. This is what is supposed to happen. I am a success at it.

Yes, there is suffering, and some self-torture, in pushing oneself to one's limits. But, of course, when it is over, there is also tremendous satisfaction, even joy, in realizing that you have done so!

So perhaps suffering and joy do go together. But the suffering comes first. The appropriate self-torture and pain must be inflicted first in order to reap the post-event reward of confidence, victory, joy (and perhaps the word is salvation). And what is salvation but redemption? It is shining, for a few glorious moments, in the radiance of joy, in joy, en-joy, or even "en-joy-ment."

But you can't consciously look or hope for joy. It is really the gift of grace, given by the higher forces as a present, a mysterious, freely bestowed reward for faithful service on the cross.

### Wednesday, July 17, 2019
### Facing Vulnerability: A Step Toward Enjoyment

How strange psychologically are these knees: How deeply they reflect my emotions. Perhaps their pain is a reflection of a subtle return to the old "cloud of impending doom" neighborhood that used to periodically hang over me. In other words, they're Sarnoian knees. Sure, they may hurt a bit. I am pushing them with lots of unaccustomed extra tour walking and additional yogic stretching. Such post-use stiffness is normal. But my psychological addictions are crippling!

If all of the above is true, and I believe it is, I should look at my knees as a psychological reaction to leading my tour with all its subtle and unsubtle responsibilities—and admit to myself how important it is that my travelers are happy!

Although I am not responsible for their happiness (I am only responsible for the effort to run the best tour I can run), when they are unhappy, it makes me unhappy.

So I want to make them happy. I do it partly, mostly, by focusing completely on every traveler and the unity of my group, for the entire tour. And I suppose that's a big weight on my head. But since I don't want to face it or put it in my head, I instead distract it, turn it away, and put it in my knees!

All this is nothing new.

So what have I learned this morning? Hopefully, to think of my knees differently. And face how important it is to me that my travelers are happy, and I will do almost anything to make them so!

My tours are very personal. I think I have never really wanted to face or realize this. I disguise it with humor, distract it with knees pain or whatever. And indeed, if making my travelers happy is so important and personal to me, then with each tour I am vulnerable. I am putting my happiness and soul on the line—much like, actually the same as, giving a concert!

So basically, nothing has changed. Only perhaps I am now more aware, more open to facing my own vulnerability, the chances I am taking, putting my teenage reaching for the Beethovian Magnificence-violin-playing soul on the line.

My escape days are over. I am diving straight into the fire! (Note my nightmare!) I am facing my (forever) vulnerability. And maybe for the first time. For the first time? But what else could the eighties be all about?

Part of my daily routine should be to thank God. A good idea.

(I sense, in this last paragraph, I am again trying to escape the positive results of my responsibilities and vulnerabilities, which include successes, by handing them to God. I also hate to face the grand feeling of personal triumph that comes with my successes. Of course, ultimately God is responsible for everything. That is a given. Still, He doesn't need the credit, but I do! I need to learn how to accept it, love it, take it. This is definitely hard for me. It belongs in the glory.)

But glory to Jim is really hard to take. And since God and man work together, which means that God and Jim work together, God cannot receive his proper glory until Jim can accept and take his own.


*Friday, July 19, 2019*
*End of Tour and Business TMS: My Aches and Pains Are Over!*

Strangely, when I stood on the Galway dock and understood the Sarnoian nature of the pains in my legs, knee, and ankles, it felt like a turning point.

I realized these "worry freezes" were TMS pains. All of them!
Then doubt stepped in as "hard to believe."
As Sarno says, doubt is one of the mind's last TMS strongholds.
So I decided to drop my doubt and absolutely believe it was TMS

pain. Which means, as pockets of oxygen deprivation, my body parts still hurt, but the hurting does no damage. And although it may sometimes hurt to an excruciating level, it "means nothing," does no damage to my body, and will eventually, suddenly, and mysteriously disappear! Which it does. I've experienced the sudden disappearance countless times.

### Stock Market Trading Money Versus Business Money

The money I make (and lose) in stock market trading is scurry-and-worry money. It is anxiety money.

But the money I make in business is firm and steady, and brings me confidence and happiness.

Trading in the stock market keeps me on edge and anxious. Truth is, on edge and anxious is where I have been all my business life. Thus, trading has reflected my business life.

### Putting My Money in a Bank

Wow! Would this mean putting my money in a bank and watching it grow at a mere earnings rate? Depending on how much I earn?

The way I used to do it in my Greenwich Village days at the St. Marks Place bank. I was so happy to watch it increase, slow and steady, with only my earnings added.

It means coming home full circle.

Back to life as an artist.

Back to my roots. But with greater knowledge, wisdom, and freedom. And the ability to run wild on the lawn of reality, the lawn of business and artistic life.

### Sunday, July 21, 2019
### Business Enters My Miracle Schedule

Business now belongs in my miracle schedule!

And a long time coming—an entire lifetime! It means my going-public self has totally come out of its violin-playing teenage years, chamber-of-imagination closet.

Wow! What an idea.

First thing that comes to mind is that my writing, my publications, are important. And that, therefore, I must not only publish more but aim to spend time and effort disseminating my work.

The very thought of this gets me sick. I am starting over, from the beginning, and again as a failure. My books have gone nowhere. Also I'm feeling a bit scared, vulnerable. Do I really dare expose myself in such a manner?

### Monday, July 22, 2019
### Suffering Is the Human Condition, and Mine, Too

Great night of dancing last night in Killarney. When I finished I even felt a glimmering of a glimmer of I-like-leading-a-tour. But, of course, in the morning, that glimmer is gone. Back to the heavy weight.

What's the big deal? Why, after all, should I enjoy my tours? Period. That's just the way it is. And nothing wrong with it.

I know this is an "Enjoy" leaf, and it's about enjoyment. But there is no enjoyment in running tours. And that's just fine. If anything, I can say that suffering, as and when I lead a tour, is my mode of "enjoyment."

### Tuesday, July 23, 2019
### Suffering is Responsibility and Vice Versa

A new concept of myself is being born on this tour, thanks to my conversation with Miriam. She said it is impossible to enjoy your job as a tour leader. Joy may come later, but not during the job. Too much responsibility.

My new concept of myself may become that I am a responsible person. And this, indeed, is my nature,

Why do I now know this? Because I now know I like to suffer. And what does suffering mean but to bear a burden, to carry my cross. (Sub-'from below' + ferre 'to bear'.) In my case, the burden of tour responsibility.

When I teach folk dancing or give a performance, all are under the rubric of responsibility of pleasing my audience. That's why I was nervous years ago and am continually nervous now before a performance of any kind, whether it be teaching, leading, or whatever. Responsibility is responsibility, burden is burden.

But I see, saw myself, my essential nature, as one of being an artist. An artist is free, childlike, uncaring of others, and essentially irresponsible. (Or was that my mother talking?) In any case, that notion of myself is over.

I now see myself as a responsible person, one who takes on and accepts burdens, and the fears and concerns that go with them. That's just the way I am. Therefore, all my pre-performance anxieties are real and necessary, good and proper, healthy and wise, and totally fitting for a responsible man but, of course, not for the irresponsible child.

Thus, I can "happily" accept my burdens: It is simply my nature.

### Sunday, July 28, 2019

Guitar, singing: The slower I go, the deeper I go, and the more I cry. I must be going somewhere, getting somewhere. But where?

I'm touching new emotional places I never dared go before, because I never dared to move, to play this slowly. I've always been under the self-pressure to play fast, move fast, do things quickly perhaps to get them over with so I could once again be "free."

But free from what? And what would I do with my new freedom?

Perhaps it's freedom from the pressure to move fast. To be free from the probing and critical eyes of the so-called public (which must, in essence, be my mother—who or what else could it be?).

What to do?

Perhaps feel the depths of my pain and pleasure.

Would I dare move so slowly in public, play guitar or even sing so slowly, and, in the process, expose my deepest feelings? Would I lose my audience by playing with such unfettered exploration? Would they simply get up and go away?

I need them to earn a living.

If I lost them, I would end up penniless and die. Thus, do I dare expose my so-called true, deeper, hidden self, so open and raw? Is it smart, wise, dangerous to reveal my vulnerable, adventurous, dreamer, and exploratory self?

### Monday, July 29, 2019

I woke up with almost excruciating lower back pain. Thus, this morning's obstacle.

Why? Too much yoga yesterday? I doubt it. The Sarnoian aspect that I finally finished my Ireland tour videos, and am "free," and the so-called trauma of emptiness and getting ready to move on? My lower back pain would be a way of keeping me in the old neighborhood of worry, fear, depression, and emptiness as forms of self-motivation.

Maybe.

But maybe, at this point, it no longer matters why. It's "just another obstacle." Every day I wake up there is another obstacle. It may be time to say "So what?"

I've had these complaints and excuses all my life. Only their "reasons" change. Now I have merely invented, created a new obstacle.

But there is an advantage that comes with age and aging, and in a sense getting wiser. Basically, in life I've "gotten somewhere." In fact, at this point, I've "gotten everywhere." I've accomplished most of the things I wanted to do. I've nowhere else to go. I want and need little.

It means doing things with no other purpose than diving straight into them, squeezing all the juices out of them, and this for no other reason than enjoying their being.

### Pain Free Existence: The No-Pains "Reality"

I started my yoga practice around 8:00 a.m. this morning, and to my amazement, no pains! I can't believe it. I'm so used to aches and pains when I start that this beginning felt unreal.

I searched for pains, even tried to create some in order to make it "real" again.

Maybe better is to accept this new "reality," that sometimes, for many reasons (even non-Sarnoian ones that I don't and never will understand), I will have no pains!

## Ego Problem and Creativity: Fictionalizing Myself

My one-man Jim Gold Show.

Somehow I hate this title.

I'm too shy and too egotistical.

It reminds me of myself and thus makes me self-conscious—like admitting, saying publically when introducing a dance, that I choreographed it.

So using my name may not be the best, most creative, way for me to go to escape my ego, step outside it.

## Just Do It and Shut Up

Don't be so awed by the above revelations.

It may have taken years for the leaf to grow. But now it has finally matured, done what it needed to do and is finished, ready to fall.

This means jump straight into the next life.

Just do it and shut up.

## Monday, August 5, 2019
## On Running, Responsibility, and Love Drawing Energy
## from an Audience: Self-Improvement

I'm put off by the hurt and fatigue of the "long" run I took yesterday at the farm. Slowly, age is draining my speed. (If not age, what else?)

Should I continue to call it running when I do it so slowly? Maybe the term "walking" is better. Evidently, that's what it looks like to outsiders. Otherwise, why would they "compliment and encourage" me by saying, "Have a nice walk."

But I even "run" slower than a walk, especially a normal walk by a younger person.

Along with running slowly yesterday, I also ran a shorter distance. And it took longer. And I didn't go down the big mountain hill partly because I knew I would have to return by coming up it, and I wasn't sure I could make it.

The only good thing about my running at this age is that I continue to do it. Or do "something" which I used to call "running."

Maybe it's time for a new name, a new term for this movement and activity.

What would I call it? (Of course, a new name will not make me run any better or faster.)

The above is definitely a negative view of a "new" running style.

Is there a positive view?

I like to run on the road to self-improvement.

What should I do?

Easy. Even in this new slowed-down, lessened, and diminished state, I could still work to improve.

What about the admiration of others? Could I draw energy from their admiration, attract inspiration from their love?

Is such a use of audience energy even worth considering?

Truth is, at any age or speed, I still love to improve.

### Thursday, August 8, 2019

Fifty years ago Alexander Bellow said my tremolo was uneven, and I could improve it by playing is slowly and evenly. I did that. . .for fifty years. I'd say it didn't work. (Plus I could play tremolo fine when I studied with Rolando Valdez-Blaine. He had a different teaching method. He just said, "Do it." And I did.

Time to return. Back to uneven, fast, and finger focus. My way!

### Wednesday, August 14, 2019
### Call to Writing

I woke up in a sudden down and empty state. I know the feeling. It is the call to writing.

It comes with a bit of an "ugh."

Why ugh? A bit of fear here.

Why?

I'm not sure.

One thing nice—this new keyboard feels so good! Perhaps replacing the old one symbolizes my return to writing. In any case, there remains a slight fear. I wonder why.

Perhaps it's partly remembrance of the old neighborhood and some of the old feelings I had while writing in it.

Old feelings, indeed. Yes, that's it. Panic, dismay escape, neurotic highs and lows, all were part of my old writing experience, especially (and only) while writing fiction.

Fiction was my escape route from business reality.

But I no longer need that escape route. So as I return to writing, it is time to reassess my entire fiction writing experience!

# New Normal

*Wednesday, October 2, 2019*
*Love*

The "I love you" goodbye:

I feel like a fool saying it. It seems mushy, untrue. Miki criticized it. She hates it. It's not part of my upbringing.

David started saying it. A great contribution, but very hard for me to say.

Can I say " I love you" to myself? Probably not. But it starts there, deep in the self. What progress I would make, if I could! Love is everywhere in my life. I just rarely acknowledge or express it. It's the beginning and end of everything. By "loving out loud," will I increase my power? Or get shot down as a fool, criticized, and belittled? I believe the former. But it is new. I'll need to try it, practice saying it.

But I've done everything else, tried everything else. There is no other place to go. I am ready to embrace love.

Over the years, I have been more focused on fear and anger.

According to Elie Wiesel, the opposite of love is indifference (not hate). The opposite of art, faith, and life too, are not ugliness, disbelief, or death, but indifference.

*Wednesday, October 9, 2019*
*Thumb and Power: Getting Used to Power, Competence, and Goodness*

What is the thumb?

What does it symbolize?

As the strongest, most manipulable finger in the hand, it means power, and symbolizes competence and goodness.

By concentrating on my thumb, I focus on my power. In doing so, I become competent and good.

Do I want to be? Can I handle it?

In the new normal world I now live in, I not only want to, I have to!

*Friday, October 11, 2019*
*A Reason to Write Fiction*

Writing fiction requires a powerful act of imagination. At the moment, thinking this way feels unnatural, untruthful, unreal.

Imagination creates reality.

I've always loved my imagination! It flourishes best in my fiction! Maybe I should write stories about my travel fears, using the wings of imagination for added elevation and to lift me out of self-inflicted miseries.

A good road to explore.

*Reading Aloud for Editing, Poetic, and Performing Purposes*

I just read *Carlos the Cloud* and ended up editing quite a bit. Reading aloud changes everything. And improves it through sound.

Will I now have to read and reread all of *Carlos* aloud before I publish? Maybe.

This is a big jump, a new editing direction. It might even push me back into performing one day, but this time as a reader.

*Wednesday, November 13, 2019*

Yesterday I went over the New Normal cliff and fell into the abyss.

I'm finally coming down from my post-Romania tour high.

But this time (hopefully) it is a little more than that. Working with Henry has really upset my equilibrium. This started when his Klezmer email list of 3,700 turned out to be a nothing. Plus, he asked me to mail it out, didn't do it himself. And after that, did absolutely nothing to publicize our tour.

Then after the tour came his questioning emails about the financial how to run my tours, etc. All total downers. Very difficult. And all the while I'm trying to decide what direction this tour should go in, whether I should work with Henry again, whether he wants to work with me. And up to now, I've been putting the final decision in his hands. I sent him a final email, giving my terms and needs, and asking if he wanted either to work with me or run his own tour. So far I haven't received an answer.

And this small space of waiting time has given me the opportunity to think on this a bit more.

And my decision now is: Instead of waiting for Henry's final answer, which may never come, I should make the final decision. And this morning my decision is: It is just too problematic working with Henry. So end it.

### Accepting the New Normal

Accepting that all the things I have accomplished are amazing, that I am amazing, and that the world I have created and has been created around me is amazing, and even that all is amazing, are no longer amazing.

It has become an accepted fact of my life.

Is this a sad thing? A loss of a beautiful way of viewing the world? Or is viewing the world that way a subtle form of denying my own God-given powers?

I'm not sure. But this is what is now happening. I have accepted wonder and amazement. Yes, it diminishes the pop and glow, at least for now. Maybe I'll find a new pop and glow. But I'm still in the boring acceptance of the amazement phase.

### Saturday, November 23, 2019

Sing my songs.

Do I dare? Yes. But in the past, I couldn't even admit I wrote them. Can't take the credit. Too much ego.

Here's the new way: I don't have to admit I wrote any of them! No one is forcing me. In fact, I like hiding behind my created names like Dmitri Zlato, Arany Janos, etc. Just as I don't have to admit I choreographed all my dances, I don't have to admit I wrote my songs, or even my stories! I can bypass my ego with all its self-consciousness and fears. Just do them! Period. No explanation. If asked, I'll say they are mine. Or someone else's, namely Dmitri Zlato, Jimenez del Oro, or another one of my characters. This is the new way. Jump past the ego self-block. Just sing them. Just dance them. Just do it!

Yes, I can do that. Let me new "Jimmy Just-Do-It" character, or Robert the Rustic Robot, or other.

### Sunday, November 24, 2019

I'm sad because Henry has talents as a speaker, writer, and organizer, plus he's funny. I'm angry because of the frustrations of working with him, his distrust, and basically doing nothing to promote our tour.

I'm disappointed because after all the time, effort, and work I put into the tour and teaching him about the tour business, it didn't work out. Result: Even if he agrees to lead a tour under my aegis, I must still say no. This to save myself from his poisons.

Thus, I have been "quietly" angry with him for almost a year, 10–11 months of quiet fury, of seething rage at Henry for doing nothing! I've been furious at him for almost a year! Well, I'm just waking up now.

### Monday, November 25, 2019
### Aftermath, Afterthoughts, After-Effects, After All

The Henry incident, working "with" him, has sucked up all my inspiration. As I look back, I ask myself: Could I have done it any differently? I don't see how. Thus, as long as I wanted to organize a Klezmer/Folk Dance Tour of Romania, there was no other way. No other Klezmer expert rose up or came to mind. When Zalman couldn't do it, there was no one left but Henry. And I thought, since Henry had organized and run his KlezKamp for so many years, he would know business, know how to advertise and get his people to register. He even offered a 3,700-person email list!

The first (and perhaps final) hint came when he said not he but I should be the one who sends out the emails from his list. As I remember, his explanation, or rationalization, was that it was my tour and it would be better coming from me. This certainly didn't sound right to me, but I didn't want to insist that he do it. Plus he said he didn't know how to send it, that his assistant did all the emails. So I contacted his assistant, worked with him, got the email list, and learned how to use MailChimp to email out all 3,700 names. I ended up emailing them about five times. Result: Three or four responses saying how nice such a tour would be. But not one registration! Then I found out that most of Henry's KlezKamp email list was old, email addresses missing and useless. Who knows how many people it actually reached.

That was my down period. I realized I was all alone in this venture, that it would be up to Lee F. to get people, and that, if they came, they would all be from my own email list. There was no way I was going to expand my market as I had originally hoped.

That was the point when I could have quit. But of course I didn't, since I had already committed myself to the tour. So I continued to promote it while quietly seething at Henry for doing nothing (and making a good profit by getting paid pretty well in the process. A free trip plus $100 per person!).

Well, the result was: we ended up with 30 people (28 paying), so that even after all expenses, I still ended up with a good profit.

So where am I this morning?

I feel like I've just been hit and run over by a tank. Okay, but it is done. I know it's time to move on. But how does one recover their inspiration?

### New Enthusiasms and Inspirations

In my Upcoming New Normal World I have to start promoting, advertising, and selling my upcoming *Treasury of International Folk Dances choreographed by Jim Gold*.

This sales approach, actually trying to sell my own book, unabashed, unashamed, un-self-conscious, and in happy exuberance is totally new!

It is part of my upcoming New Normal world.

Wow!

To do so is a major mental and psychological accomplishment. It is something I have never done, or been able to do.

Imagine, to have love and enthusiasm for my own work. (Well, I've always had it, but only in *secret*.)

### Tuesday, November 26, 2019

Deep sadness this morning as I am not fulfilling the promises I made to myself.

As I say, the inspirations and directions I had before my Romanian tour have all but disappeared. Feels like I've somewhat lost my way and can't get back on track. I had it all together before the tour. Now, I'm drained and lost.

Is this true? Or is it a mere "feeling"? No doubt the latter. But still, I must deal with it.

I like dealing with the repercussions of success.

Why do I feel successful?

Money is good, the tour was good, article in the *Jewish Standard* was good, finishing and upcoming publishing of my choreo book are good. My life is mostly in order. Lot of goods here.

But lots of goods mean lots of endings. I'm finished with my choreo book, finished with my Romania tour, and the stock market speculation in small and penny stocks seems to have also come to a close. Seems I even succeeded there, that is, since I've lost so much money in the penny stock process, I've succeeded in giving up my hopes for their quick and instant rises. So that hope and pleasure is also gone.

### Friday, November 29, 2019
### *Remembering Balance*

Is my miracle schedule more important than my business? No. But my miracle schedule is the foundation of my business. And no house can stand without a foundation, and a foundation is useless without a house. I must do both. But I must start with my foundation.

*Monday, December 2, 2019*
### Directing Energy

It seems that the "natural" tendency of energy is downward. Gravity pulls it toward the earth. This certainly seems true of mental energy.

If not given something higher to aim for, the mind slants earthward, downward. That's why the best attitude and approach is to each day aim to do better than the day before. This philosophy directs the energy upward, away from depression and toward joy.

What did I do yesterday to make my day better than the day before? I added squats and guitar playing.

### Two Great Questions

1. Am I on the (creative) path to something absolutely marvelous or to something absolutely mediocre? Artists create. I am an artist. Artists are on the creative path and the creative path can only lead to something absolutely marvelous. (Otherwise it is not the creative path.)

2. What "impossible" thing am I believing or planning for? A beautiful "Alhambra" and excellent knees. I'm on the path. I could live in the land of the Marvelous "Alhambra." Knees, too. I could live in the land of excellent knees. I just added squats.

This could be the New Normal.

### Let Curiosity Win

I have to let myself into this new land. I have to allow myself in. I need permission. My own permission. Why do I need it? I don't know.

Maybe I'm afraid to enter. Fear it. It's strange, unknown, I'm not used to it. All possible, and probably true. But so what? I'm there now.

## A Land of Optimism and Joy

Does such a land really exist?

Doubts are coming back. I'm slipping. . .back into "reality," or at least the old familiar reality.

But this is a new land, a place I'm familiar with because I've visited it temporarily. But I've never made it my "permanent" residence as we have done in Teaneck.

So now I must give up my doubts and move in. Give it a try. See what happens. Let curiosity win.

That's what this break between tours is for, this "vacation" period. To find a new experimental place to live and give it a try.

Moving is possible. But changing residence is more difficult than I thought. There is so much furniture to either bring or replace.

It will take time, and getting used to the new neighborhood.

## Function and Purpose of Trading Penny Stocks

Maybe penny stocks are my form of play. Maybe I need to trade them as my form of play. And since I need to play that way, I can at least try to keep my losses low. Maybe trading penny stocks is one of my "hobbies," my needs, and thus one of my expenses.

## Wednesday, December 4, 2019
## Art and Commerce

Sales pushed me out of myself and forced me to relate to people. Art is a higher calling, but without sales, I might end up alone, high upstairs, in the closet, lost and isolated in my artistic garret, writing the great American novel.

The happy result of sales is money. And money both protects and excites me. Money buys safety. But it also brings power and excitement. Thus, sadly it seems, sales and money push me to connect to people.

Sales connect me to the outside world. Along with the money they dump into my coffers, they bring me safety, power, connection, and excitement. Yet I always feel it is a higher calling, and this even though creating it isolates me.

Ideally, I would create art in order to bring it to people, to "sell" it to them. And in truth, this is what I do.

However, I always (used to) feel a grand separation between art and business, between creation, the highest form that can be, and sales with the money they bring in.

I can explain this separation and the disdain I feel for sales and money as having been caused by my upbringing. These indeed seemed to be my parents' values. "Seemed," I say, because maybe deep down, they weren't. After all, my parents were both public school teachers and principals and thus had a steady, secure job.

I have never had one. I always wanted and needed security, but I never wanted to attain it that way. The artistic life was the one for me, and this was all the heroism of its insecurity. And that's the life I chose.

Luckily, I also had to make money, which forced me out of my cocoon to meet and deal with the public.

So I am definitely a split personality, divided between art and commerce, ever worshiping art while disdaining sales and money. The only "improvement" I can see in my attitude is that I disdain them less than I used to. Wouldn't it be nice if I could love and worship sales (and money) along with art, unite them into one grand world ball? Wouldn't it be nice if I could turn schizophrenia into monophrenia?

But though I have made "progress" on this attitude and issue, I am still not there yet. My New Normal Land is still in conflict.

I know intellectually that art and commerce go together, that on a higher, the highest, of levels, they are one. But intellect and emotions have yet to fuse. Once in a while it happens, but it is rare.


*Thursday, December 5, 2019*
*Happiness, Bliss, Wisdom: Remembering and Maintaining*
*the Yogic Trance State*

I'm not there yet.
A sudden chill of happiness burst through my veins.

How do I arrive at, maintain, and remember such a high state of vision? It is a godly yogic trance state. But I don't have the expertise yet to maintain or remember it. I'm not there.

I can know, and even maintain it for a few seconds, maybe, if I'm lucky, even a minute. But how to build it up over long periods? That is the question, and no doubt, biggest life challenge.

## The Attitude

The attitude is the substratum, the base, the bottom; it is also the top, the pinnacle, the ultimate height and connection, the yogic trance state. It's not about money, leading tours, former folk dance weekends, dance classes, security, stocks, or day trading, It's not even about worldly fears and short-term accomplishments or temporary goals. It's what yogis call bliss. Others call it God, Reality, Nirvana; I'll call it The Attitude.

Everything else is below The Attitude. In a sense, all that is beside the point. "Beside it," next to the Point, on the side of it, secondary, vaguely seen, pleasantly envisioned, but not bottom-line.

## Friday, December 6, 2019
### A Visit with Divine Madness: Benefits of Falling off the Cliff

I went deep into myself, so deep that I fell off a cliff, and, in the process, lost the world. Now I'm back. What happened? Why?

First, what did I gain? What benefits accrued to me? If any? Well, on guitar I gained big time and mucho. Was it temporary? I hope not. We'll see. How did I reach that point?

I'm not sure. But part of it was the "I don't give a damn" feeling, I'm playing as fast as I can, and fuck the world; all my internal and external critics can go to hell. Yes, I guess I was angry, maybe furious. A divine madness descended upon me, and in that process, I succeeded. At least temporarily. I said "Fuck 'em all," and (as a result?) my guitar playing just flew! It was totally great. I had days of amazement and awe. Truly, I was in another world, a world of shining power and glory.

But to get there, I had to temporarily leave this world. My wings were made of divine madness. Now, after a session with Rick, I'm back.

## My Thanksgiving Gift: Divine Madness

This brief visit was a result of the vacation I needed and promised to take after my Romania tour ended. I knew I had a spot of down time from mid-November to January with no tour or sales pressure.

It took two or three weeks to recover from Romania. This put me almost exactly into Thanksgiving "vacation" time. And that's when I gave myself the vacation from everyone and everything, which included the internal freedom to receive the gift of divine madness that descended into my fingers and spread immediately to my guitar playing.

It felt vaguely like rage but a bit beyond that, too.

Now I'll simply try to be thankful and appreciate my gift. After all, it was Thanksgiving.


## Return

I return to Earth. And with my return come earthly self-doubts: Is the biblical creation story true, or merely a myth? Did divine madness really descend upon me? Am I worthy of such visit? Did it really happen? Is man really a semi-divine creature? Am I?


## What is Divine Madness?

What is divine madness? It feels like anger, a quiet fury building.

But it is more than that. Slowly the mind seems to shrink under a (thunder) storm of blinding rage. Maybe rage is needed to energize the soul, toughen it, push it beyond daily fragility, and give it the power to break earthly bonds, and thus open itself to higher powers. Isn't that what just happened to me? If it did, I am so privileged!


## Saturday, December 7, 2019

Driving home from my Darien folk dance class, I was in some kind of panic. I didn't quite understand why. I sensed it had something to do with the combination of fright and glory that divine madness brings.

The fright, really a terror and panic, comes from the loss of control that takes place when you jump off the cliff and fall, float, or fly over the chasm, the abyss. The glory and wonder come when you "finish your event," in other words, transcend it and feel the joy of accomplishment.

That's what I felt after the folk dance class. Despite my fears, aches and pains, worries about making it through another night, I again managed to run a great dance class, a party really. Everyone had a great time, including me! And although after the class I could hardly walk and was ready to hobble to my car and home, I decided to fall to the floor and go through a yoga stretching routine. I ended up twisting and extending for a half hour which almost immediately brought wonders of love and relaxation to my body: Slowly all my muscles loosened, the aches and pains dribbled away. I ended up loose and smiling and, after a minute of dead pose, happily and easily made my way  home!

### The Blessings of Anonymity

There's the expectation that publishing *Carlos the Cloud* and *A Treasury of International Folk Dances* choreography book will somehow dramatically change my life. Truth is, publishing my book was hardly noticeable and changed just about nothing. Same thing with the *Jewish Standard* article on my Romania tour. Except for a momentary blip of wild interest, nothing much has moved.

This is surprising, disturbing, relieving, and calming. In a sense, maintaining my anonymity frees me. When I am not noticed, the pressure is off. Absence of fame, remaining unnoticed and unknown, are a back door blessing and a cheap way to purchase freedom.

### Sunday, December 8, 2019
### One Doorway at a Time: Thumb, Confidence, and Power

I am hoping my path of self-denial is coming to an end, that my thumb can overcome and open the door to laughing sunshine, glorious, high-minded amazement, happiness, even worship. Yes, a bit of self-worship or worship by others wouldn't hurt. . .but again I must ask, if it came now, could I take it? Or would I push it away, deny it, and move back into my protective violin chamber, the shielded cave that guards me from the sunshine of glory?

Note the blinding headache that just hit me.

### Tired of Hiding

I'm tired of hiding. Maybe that's been the cause of my grand fatigue.

After so many years of struggle, my walls have finally collapsed. Nothing left to do but see my creations as good for others, helping others, healing them.

The strange thing is that, deep in my heart, *I do believe* they do. My choreographies heal others. True also for my books, songs, classical guitar playing, folk tours, weekends, and guitar lessons. In fact, almost everything I do brings good things to others.

Now I just have to practice training my mind to remember it.

### On Selling My Books

I won't make much money from my book sales. Then why sell them? If there is no or so little money in it, why even try? (I can make more money selling tours.)

Because if I don't try, put in the effort, I get a headache and nausea, followed by a feeling of self-disgust.

Result: It's bad when I sell, but worse when I don't.

### Monday, December 9, 2019

I have to *like* it. If I do, some others will, too. But making the jump to the thought that others will like it, and beyond that, even if they *don't like it, it is still* good for them, will help them, is a giant leap for me. It feels arrogant, smacks of hubris. How dare I make such a claim?

The truth is I'll never know if it helps or is good for them. I can only imagine the answer. But I do know it is good for me to imagine what I do helps them.

Am I putting myself down by saying can I fool myself this way? Yes. But perhaps my arrogance is simply a form of self-protection against. . . what? Recognition of God-given talents and skills. Is it a protection against my better self? Are put-downs, seeing myself as arrogant by claiming that my creations can help and cure others really a form of self-protection?

From what? A slip over the cliff into hubris. Maybe I'm right to protect myself by putting myself down, to limit the scope of possible expansive insanity. This is also a danger. Yet to a certain degree, what I create is good for others. So maybe it's a question of judgement and degree.

## My Books

Like my children, my books are born and enter the world on their own. Soon they are not my books anymore, as they forge their own identity. I can only display and be proud of them. But they must speak for themselves.

# Beyond the New Normal

*Wednesday, December 11, 2019*
*Sales Dilemma*

When I got married, I hated sales. I forced myself to sell my "World of Guitar" assembly program to elementary and high schools because, if I didn't, I'd have to "work for a living," which, to me, meant doing something I detested, namely becoming a teacher in the New York City school system or taking a corporate job. Since I wanted to be an artist, and my wife insisted I earn a living, and I earned nothing living in my fifth floor walk-up St Marks Place apartment in the East Village, trying to write my great American novel, my money-making marriage "compromise" was to sell my guitar program. But I always hoped someday I'd make enough money that I would no longer be forced to sell.

Strangely, now, many years later, I am at that point. Although we must cut back a bit, we still have enough to survive. And I no longer have to sell! In that sense, I have succeeded.

But this does not solve my book-promoting problem.

My dream has always been to be a writer. I believe most of my best self lies in my books. And I want people to read them, and get to know the real me! But if I hate selling and no longer have to do it, how will I promote my books? I have to find *another reason* to sell, one that has nothing to do with money.

This certainly shows that money cannot buy happiness.

One positive outcome from sales is that I feel *glorious* when I sell something! When someone mails me a check, it's love in the mail. God has shone down on me.

In the past, that has never been enough to justify a sales effort. But maybe there is a higher cosmic purpose. Perhaps I've been forced to sell all along because the Big Boss knows that, despite my resistant, opposi-tional personality, sales are good for me.

How about selling for the "privilege" of exposing my essence to others, for the honor and pleasure of receiving their criticism, love, in-terest, indifference, or fascination?

## Sales and Rejection

What are sales about?

Maybe my hatred of them is simply about rejection: I just don't want to get hurt.

And yet life is full of pain. There is no escape, only avoidance and denial. What can you do? Either stay on the side, or fight. Dive in, seize the pain, ride it to the end. Then finish with a victory or two en route.

Either way you end up feeling pain. But love, inspiration, and cou-rage run the world. Diving in is a better choice.

I woke up furious at myself. Why? I've been beating my brain since Thanksgiving. Something about publishing.

Bottom line: I've forgotten how to enjoy publishing, promoting, and advertising my work.

I'm onto the problem.

When I play guitar, I love touching, feeling, plucking the string, then watching the round sound trickle out and tickle the universe around me; in books, I love hearing my writing read to the class by Barry, and lux-uriating in how others react. These things and more warm my heart in a friendly, fulfilling chuckle, a bubble of fulfillment.

There is so much pleasure to be found in what I do. I've just forgotten how to find it.

## Lost and Found Department

I've lost track of my heart, soul, mind, body, all the good parts, lost my way, been totally distracted.

I was worried about giving to others, how to improve the world by improving myself, giving of myself, etc. Ridiculous! Screw the world!

If I can't give myself pleasure, the world will be a worse place. The only way I can help the world, or anyone else, is by learning how to give myself pleasure first. It's got to start with me.

How did I get so lost? I don't know. And I don't even care. The point is to get back on track.

Perhaps publishing my book threw me off. Once *Treasury of International Folk Dances* with my choreographies came out, I was immediately slipped into the old-neighborhood pressure cooker cesspool with its I-must-now-sell-my-book compulsions. The result: a grand bout of nausea, headache, sickness and self-destruction. I didn't want to go backward, but I did anyway. Perhaps I needed to revisit old straight-jacketed ways, do them over so I could finally get it right. In other words, destroy old negatives and replace them with new pleasure-loving ones.

Finding such a new and happy self among my books would be a major accomplishment. Today I sense I'm on my way. I can start by asking the right questions.

*Monday, December 16, 2019*
*The Genesis of Amazement: Politics/History*

Politics is the art and importance of the present. History is the art and importance of the past. Dealing in politics makes history important, and dealing with history makes politics important. By stepping into the present, I embrace, crystallize, and enlarge the past.

This is a complicated way of saying structural changes have just taken place.

It started last night. I usually feel down when a project ends. Such vacuums confront me with the great emptiness question: "What's next?"

Okay, what had I finished? Basically, I had said that, once my Romania tour was finished, I'd work on my books, namely my choreo book and short story book. Well, guess what? I've been editing my *Treasury of International Folk Dances,* and now it is published and finished. My *Carlos the Cloud* book is close to finished as well.

Then I faced the usual post-publication dilemma: How to promote, advertise and sell my books? A grand bout of headaches, stomach aches, and nausea followed. And during this short period (helped by Rick), I realized I do not want, will not want, and never have wanted to promote, advertise, and sell my books! Sure, I wish others would buy them, but I don't want to put the effort and time into promotion. In fact, once they are published, in my mind they're done, and it is time to move on to the next project.

Presently, most of my past books remain in my basement. That seems to be their proper place. My secret hope is that they will be discovered by posterity. Or perhaps, more realistically, they will be completely forgotten, washed away by the flow of events, covered by the mist of years, centuries, lost in the dustbin of history.

Just as body and memories of me will disappear into the maw of time, so will my books. Sad to contemplate, but that doesn't make it less true. In any case, I've made my peace with this idea.

Okay, that was step one. Now what?

Through the cleansing process of depression, my mind has been cleared. Space has been created for something new to rush in. And this morning, it did! What? Politics! And a short bit later, History followed. Amazing. But it feels right. Also, with this new entry, suddenly the study of languages appeared! We'll see where this leads.

### Tuesday, December 17, 2019
### Success and Real Success!

I need a new big dream. All my old dreams have been achieved on some level.

Then this morning I realized I don't need new dreams. I still haven't fulfilled my old ones! I've only *given up on them!* Why? Mostly I "suffer" from victory. Tours have been successful. So has the money. I'm satisfied temporarily.

But victory and success also bring sorrow and arrogance. The arrogance protects me from the sadness of ending. But the brief joy at the top of the mountain is not a permanent place. Success, although pleasant, even glorious, is not an ending, nor an end-in-itself.

Now I'm sliding downhill on the other side of my mountain, smiling in the sunshine. Why am I happy? I'm on my way to the next mountain! That is *real* success.

*Thursday, December 19, 2019*
*Performing for Nothing, Performing for Free*

Could performing for free be the first crack? Will it make a difference? It certainly would catapult my New Normal into the stratosphere. And it has already happened in Barry's class, along with his help. But of course, I was ready.

Performing is a big fear. But why? Even in asking the question, the fear immediately diminished. I can no longer think of a reason! Somehow the reason, and with it the fear itself, has fallen out of me.

Imagine performing for nothing, for free! The idea opens the door to the possibility, hope, and even desire, of enjoying it!

I might be able to drop pre-performance anxiety.

More important, can I now begin performing again on guitar, singing, and even do readings? How about putting them all together in a one-man show?

*Friday, December 20, 2019*
*Performance: A Seismic Shift*

Being no longer afraid to perform has released strange venoms and odors. I now face the world as a free human being. I don't *have to* do anything. This enables me to ask the bottom-line philosophical question: What do I really want?

I am at the place of no purpose, meaning, or desire whatsoever. Totally empty. Plus I have another total weekend off! This after whole Xmas vacation.

Why do I want to experience an epoch of total free time, with absolutely nothing to do, not a pressure or desire in the world?

Because I want to find out if, in the depths of my emptiness, there is actually anything I really want. Beyond the basics of food, clothing, shelter, is there anything I really need? I will get to know myself, my real self. When I am un-pushed, have no outside demands; what desire deep in my core, will motivate me?

How long can it go on without purpose or meaning? Do I want to live that way? Is it even possible? Do I need to merely fill up empty time on Earth? Or is there an actual purpose to my existence, a real meaning to my life?

Fearless performance also extends to meeting people, dealing with them, leaving the house, functioning in society, and exiting the post-Covid hermit life.

But I don't want to forget the soaring high of spiritual journey, visits to the mountain top, visions of the Magnificence.

## Imagining a New Audience

Here's my new job: Imagine a naïve new audience into existence. To watch and appreciate everything I do. What does naive mean? Open to anything I play, dance, write, or do. I create audiences out of my imagination. They exist because of my imagination. In order to imagine a new audience, I must kick out the old one.

## Saturday, December 21, 2019
## Index Finger Walks on Stage

He's the big guy standing at the concert hall door, guarding and blocking my index finger. Do guarding and blocking go together? Together they create "stuck." Is my index finger stuck in the door?

Somehow, I need a metamorphosis, to be transformed, fused into one hand of liberty, given a "free hand," so my index can walk with easy flow through the door.

But the finger needs to be safe and protected.

Protected against what? The arrows of criticism, darts of negativity, deadly poisons of jealously, envy, and hatred, and all the other boulder landslides that can fall on and roll over a concert soloist.

But my naive new audience is now part of my index fan club: supporters, protector, defenders, energizers. No longer does index need to worry. It can enter the hall safely, mount the stage—and when it does, its playing will be loved and embraced.

## Monday, December 23, 2019
### Devil's Bargain

The strange Devil's bargain: I can play guitar, but I can't walk. In other words, my guitar fingers work, but in exchange, my dancing legs don't. Do I want that? Maybe for a week. I'm totally off. No dancing, no gym, no "need" to exercise, no nothing. I'm free to play guitar gloriously as I fall apart.

We'll have to see where all this leads. But for now, until the glory guitar-playing habit is established, I don't mind trading it in for hurting legs. Besides, lots of sitting is needed to play guitar well.

And to play guitar well is so *wonderful!* Flowing and weaving through classical masterpieces by Tarrega, Milan, Bach, and Sor. Add a Renaissance dance now and then.

What could be better? Maybe playing this mental game with the devil is okay for a few days. I don't mind giving up walking at all. However, I want to keep my legs functioning, along with my arms, shoulders, back, and other body parts, so we can all celebrate this glorious new guitar endeavor together.

## Wednesday, December 25, 2019

Christmas day. In Spain, in October 2018, I recognized my mortality bottom. Shadows and fears of death haunted my mind. Of course, I tried to deny them. But my body rebelled against the denial and created a distracting knee pain.

When I told Rick about it, he said I was totally stiff and needed to make my new religion one of stretching. I agreed, and began an intense stretching program of two hours a day. And it worked! Slowly my body improved. It all came down to a simple truth: When I stretched, I felt better; when I didn't, I got stiff, and felt worse.

*Friday, December 27, 2019*
*The Fun Factor*

Is the purpose and meaning of life to enjoy oneself? And the world around us? What else could it be? That means the hero is one who can enjoy himself, or herself, despite all the suffering, hardships, aches, pains, hurts, and heartaches the world imposes upon us. So focus on the fun factor. Make enjoyment a practice.

*Tuesday, December 31, 2019*
*Flirting with Disaster*

I don't want disaster. But it's stimulating to flirt with it. Curiosity? Uncertainty? Testing limits? Lack of faith? How far can I go without destroying myself?

I attribute this flirting to lack of faith. After all, why test limits if I know the future? The very nature of faith is based on "I don't know." And there are so many things I don't know. I hope my faith grows, improves. But meanwhile, I remain daring and wild, drawn to the word "if," with its tests and experiments.

*Thursday, January 2, 2020*
*Never Overwhelmed? Maybe*

Woke up this morning with a bad knee, bad back, and bad start. I know it has to do with going back to work today. And this after my great two-week "vacation." Rage and anger at my return. The usual. And this is subtly causing my morning aches and pains. But do I still need them? Everything ahead of me looks good. So basically, I'm being overwhelmed by the good. The stock market is up this morning. I can't wait for it to open in a few hours! I'm so excited! (Note bad knee, back, etc.) So I can see my left knee as my "excited knee." My back as my "excited back."

I've repressed the excitement by being overwhelmed.

I've invented overwhelmed to suppress my excitement, a self-containment against joy and fun. Am I really overwhelmed? No. I always manage to handle my situations. So I am excited—but hiding it by my own invention.

Now looking back, I wonder if I have ever really been overwhelmed. Maybe I have just been excited all the time, even over-excited, but controlling it, hiding it, through this guard-rail mechanism.

### Friday, January 3, 2020
### Doing Something by Doing Nothing

Today is a down day in the market. My market plan was to actively watch and wait for week before I did anything. But also to remain "flexible."

I am learning how to do something by doing nothing. "Actively watch and wait" means being like a tiger about to pounce. It means watching and waiting while deciding. The decision part is the active part. You're ready to instantly change your mind, depending upon circumstances.

### Business Adds Motivation

Time is precious. I have so little of it. Since this is so, what will motivate me to call folks on my email list or, for that matter, even my friends? One reason would be to grow my tour and folk dance following. But that sounds very self-serving—because it is. But obviously, it is a good thing when I call others. And the goodness remains whether the reason is self-serving or not.

Business is a positive motivator. It pushes me out of the house and into the world! If this is true, why do I always resist? Inward reticence? Fear? Desire to stay in the safe, womb-like confines of my house?

Forcing myself to do it may be the only way I ever will. And what better way of forcing myself than through the self-serving attitude of business? I can even see my work as my father telling me to stop practicing violin, get some sunshine, go play with your friends, while my mother encourages me to keep improve my art, and remain in my protective practicing womb-room.

*Business is a father to me.* An interesting, sweet way of putting it. It helps me remember him every day. What a beautiful idea. Yet note the rise of a headache as he is introduced into the picture. I remember a blinding headache as I rode down to Hamden with Miki in the back of our truck. I didn't know why. Hidden rage? I want to remember my father, relate him to my business, my strength.

He was the gateway to a positive view of business. After many years, the conflict between my inner Ma and Pa, art and business, has been resolved. No more fighting. They are united. A great attitude and psychological leap forward.

## My Study and Connection of Hebrew

The study of Hebrew connects me to God and Eternity, and to eternal life. Just what I want.

Death is something I don't want. Thus, studying Hebrew is a good way to fight death. It might not help my body, which will disintegrate on its own. But it will calm my mind, and certainly motivate and inspire my spirit.

Not a bad way to welcome the sunrise.

## Tuesday, January 7, 2020
## Improvement Is My Goal

Every day I try to climb Jacob's ladder to improve myself. On the days I don't, I feel empty and hollow.

Paradoxically, could this vacuum be caused by success?

Maybe. But perhaps instead of using the word "success" I should use "finished" or "completed."

But whatever word I use, truth is, I like to improve. In fact, I love it! Why? It's good for me. Period. Improvement inspires me to improve even more. Fun, sparkling, a good-in-itself. Opposite improvement is emptiness. And I can improve in anything I choose.

I just have to do it.

*Wednesday, January 8, 2020*
*Eternity*

I need eternity to give my life long-term meaning. Thus, I need God. (Whether He needs me is another question.) The fact that I need Him for permanence is a good enough reason for His existence.

With everything around me, including myself, transient, I need the existence of an infinite source. (Doesn't everybody? How do you find meaning without it?)

*Saturday, January 18, 2020*
*Enjoy the Moment*

Although I feel successful this morning, I can't say I enjoy the feeling. But I don't dislike it either. I'm more in shock than anything else. I don't know what to do with this new self-image. Be thankful and leave it at that? See it as a pleasant passing phenomenon, a good day? Probably, the latter is best. In fact, part of this questioning is to avoid the happy feeling of pleasantness.

Indeed, best is to jump into it, let it settle in my bones, swish around my body, bring a dopamine massage of joy to my brain, let it do its thing . . .and then let it pass. That's the wise and smart way to handle a day of success.

### What Do I Need?

I need my body. So I keep it in shape. I need my voice. So I practice singing. But do I need my guitar?

The answer is: You live for love and beauty. What else is there? What else could be better?

So yes, I need my guitar!

### I Am a Gambler

I like risk. Not too much but enough to stimulate my brain. However, the risk I took with LK was just too big. Too much money to gain or lose. And I am in the process of losing most of it. I have to sell down the stock to a comfort level and stimulation balance, then put in a stop loss and hope I don't need it.

Gambling is my vice-hobby. I have the mild gambler mentality. But only in the stock market. Maybe I should read up about gamblers and speculators, get to know more people like myself.

Can I find a challenge to replace gambling? Or am I addicted? If I am, is it a skill I can learn? Should I "study" small stock speculation? Is it worth trying to improve my trading skill? Or is it more worthwhile trying to give it up? Or simply see my trading venture as a passing storm cloud, pay it little attention, and move on?

On the other hand, what challenge could really absorb my mind?

Dare I say I'm trading stocks to avoid writing and promoting my books? Such a major effort means public appearances, readings, maybe even radio and TV appearances. All in order to push and promote my books. A scary effort filled with rejection possibilities.

## Monday, January 27, 2020
### Remembering Who I Am

I never thought much about money before marriage. After marriage, I thought almost only about money. Since then, my obsession with earning a living has never stopped. Most of it is to impress my wife. Sure, I need some money for myself, but most, the excess security part, is for her, to make her happy. In fact, I would even say my stock market speculating and trading are just another way of trying to impress her with my money-making skills. And this, even as I lose money in the process.

(There's also the thought that God has a sense of humor since my trading skills are so laughable.)

I don't blame her for my money-making obsession. She wants financial security through money, and so do I. Of course, the obsession part comes from me.

I really need a new self-definition. Actually, I could remind myself of my old self-definition, the one I discovered as teenager and in my first dreamy year of college at the University of Rochester: A self-definition based on love of learning and self-improvement. What did I love? Violin, basketball, study. Not that I got good grades. They were terrible. But I loved the study process, the magnificence of learning, the adventure of reading a book, letting the universe open and expand before me, and dwelling in marvels.

Let remembering who I was become remembering who I am.

*Tuesday, February 4, 2020*
*Life as a Fool*

What have I learned? Maybe what I saw as a defeat is really a re-treat. Maybe I just can't give up. It's not in my personality. Giving up to me is death. Thus, I cannot give up trading. I *can* do it "differently," especially after being chastened by this historic retreat.

Retreat is a mental state, an attitude. So is defeat. Evidently, my personality, and even character, are: Retreat yes, defeat no. I feel a bit like a fool. But after accepting fool status, I feel a bit better already!

Life as a fool may be the smart, realistic, humble, best, and wise way to go.

# Next
# Stage

# The Next Stage: Exhilaration, Joy, Ecstasy

*Monday, February 10, 2020*
*Hard on Myself*

I like being hard on myself. That means pushing myself, forcing myself to follow my disciplines. When I do, I feel great! When I don't, I feel pointless and empty, that I've wasted my day, my evening, my time, sick, a bit nauseous, disgusted, unfulfilled, and awful.

This morning I'm happy and satisfied. But I also feel pressured. I want to repeat yesterday's victories. Although yesterday, with all its wonders, is dead, I am tied to its splendor and glory.

So, rather than actually being here this morning, I am dwelling on the wonders of yesterday, clinging to the far-away past. I'm not free to dive into the only reality that exists, the stream of today's present.

I like the process of learning. And memories of yesterday's learning are nice.

But clinging to them is unpleasant. And the only fix for this dilemma is self-awareness.

*Miracle Schedule Life Style*

Here is a completely opposite view: Could it be that my life, my daily miracle schedule activities, are so interesting that even performances by virtuosos cannot surpass them? That so-called "outside stimulation," although possibly pleasant, is no longer necessary? In fact, even its so-called "pleasantness" feels a bit like a waste of time. Why waste my time like that when I can do things that are inspiring and great. . .such as those I do in my daily life?

In fact, just thinking is itself very inspiring. Could the above be my reason for last night's disappointment?  Is it total hubris to say my life is so good, fascinating, even fun?  Is it a daring thing to say?  Is it true?  I'm afraid it is. Then why be afraid?  Perhaps I need not be.

Admit living in the light is my way of creating miracles daily, even hourly.

Although virtuosos like Andy Statman are their own miracle, my miracles, although different, are just as good.  (And perhaps, since they are my own, even better.)

### Crumbling of a World View

Maybe virtuosity itself, although glorious, is not enough. Like a grand tickle, it's pleasant, but I don't need it to touch heaven.  Following the miracles in my schedule may be enough.

My old world view is crumbling. No wonder the concert upset me. Now I see the virtuosity I thought I needed to play "Alhambra" fast is no longer needed. I'm wasting time practicing to become a virtuoso.

I no longer have to worship speed.  During this recent earthquake, I've outgrown it. I'm changing religion from Fast to Slower.  This is cause for celebration. Freed of my speed and virtuoso chains, I can relish in my new guitar-playing freedom.

Virtuosity used to pound my ego.  And some of it leaked into my soul.  (Today, it still affects me, but hopefully a bit less).  But today I have also created a space beyond for the blue sky of a schedule in which I can peek into, and even enter, my soul.

### Tuesday, February 11, 2020

Love is located within. Somehow I lose or bypass it, when focusing on pleasing others.

Divine selfishness is the way to go.  Please yourself first.  As the sun shines within, it soon shines outward, lights up the room, as others bathe in your sunlight.

And they smile as you leave, waving goodbye, as you jaunt along singing upbeat songs with occasional choruses of Hebrew hallelujahs.

*Thursday, February 13, 2020*
*The Grand Purpose*

Nothing has changed. But everything has changed. I am suddenly invested with a grand and great purpose.

Of course, it's really not so sudden. I knew my purpose all along. But somehow I was not ready to plunge into it yet.

Now there is no denying it. Putting off is no longer a choice. I am ready.

Just do it!

Amazing how actually *doing it* changes my mood.

*Sunday, February 16, 2020*
*Guitar Discovery*

Guitar: Planting the hypothenar relaxation flag more deeply in my bass thumb. Slower focus. Do I dare to go slow again? Yes. But not on a deeper relaxation level. In today's process, I am moving (have moved) from tough-structure hypothenar muscle to the more fluid V-shaped, web-shaped connector area between hypothenar and thumb, the fluid middle ground.

The index finger is related to that web-shaped connector. Actually, I am discovering a new sector of my right hand. No one can confirm its truth or value but me.

An hour later, this discovery brings me a beautiful relaxed tone on the guitar, and a deep feeling of peace and security.

*Heavenly Guitar Playing*

It takes energy and years. I'm pushing a flow of large joy chips through a tiny space in my right wrist.

On the other side is heaven.

Once I'm through, clouds will pass, the sky will open, and my guitar playing will be heavenly!

The devil is on the run.

Diving into toil, trouble, and danger, falling through the *Alice in Wonderland* right wrist, I'll slide into guitar-playing heaven.

### Monday, February 17, 2020
### Deeper

My world is getting smaller and smaller, narrower and narrower; I'm concentrating on fewer and fewer areas, focusing on less and less. I'm heading deeper, down rather than sideways, vertical rather than horizontal. It's the wisdom part of aging.

Seems my biggest challenge now is disintegration of body parts, disability, and death. Not a happy challenge but a challenge nevertheless. Maintenance is the word. Going backward means moving forward. If I can do, consciously and with difficulty, what I used to do easily and without thinking, that's progress.

Okay, done. Now it's time to dive back into the daily distractions of this world.

### Improving as a Good-In-Itself

I may never play guitar in public again. And that's fine. I like the practice process. I do it because I want to get better. I have no other goal in mind. Practicing guitar, along with improving and getting better, is a good-in-itself. That may be all I need now. It may be enough.

The desire to perform and show others my accomplishments is fading. It seems beside the point. Evidently, I don't have enough desire, energy, or interest to set up a show outside my living room practice.

If I ever perform again, anywhere or on any instrument or in any style, it would have to be for an entirely different purpose. Otherwise, I just won't bother.

Is exhilaration a good new reason?

I'd say yes. In fact, I'd say that exhilaration is the only reason to ever perform again.

Would a performance on classical guitar exhilarate me? How about singing folk songs? Or the combination *Jim Gold Show* of guitar, folk songs, gaida, ad libs, humor, and spontaneity?  Or becoming a comedian, seeing my show as a stand-up comic routine? Maybe.  After all, I like "off the wall," crazy, wild, nutty, and fantasy. Maybe this kind of smorgasbord show is the way to go.

### Exhilaration Maintenance

The word "fun" seems too childish, weak, and superficial to describe what I want out of life.  Better are exhilaration, joy, ecstasy, transformation, majesty, humor, and Magnificence.  These glorious states of mind are the best antidotes to death, disability, transience, and depression.

How to achieve and maintain them? That is the question.

### The Joy Point

The relaxation point in my right wrist is the joy point for my guitar playing!  When focusing on its release, easy flow and beauty follows, and I can approach the perfection point I need.

Searching for that guitar ecstasy spot has taken me a lifetime. This morning, for a few glorious moments, I found it.

### Folk Dancing

I often hit the exhilaration spot while I'm teaching my folk dance classes and dancing along with everyone else. It all feels so easy and natural for me.  Maybe that's why it is my profession, even if it doesn't pay.

### Wednesday, February 19, 2020

I have it.  I've always had it.  It has always been there.

But I must re-find and reclaim it every day.  Every morning begins with a difference, and you have to steer the ship anew.

Play guitar and exercise: Isn't that my ideal life?  Just as in my teenage years, when I discovered music and exercise, the source of happiness.

Uniting body, mind, and spirit. Music focuses my mind and spirit; exercise tunes my body. And when they work together, their perfect combination equals happiness.

*Monday, February 24, 2020*
*Feelings*

I usually feel defeat when I have feelings of sadness, depression, whatever, these so-called negative feelings. But rather than defeated, better to see them as clouds passing in the night.

True, they can be storm clouds raining down destruction and pain, or clear sky and sunlight feelings bringing uplift and joy.

But clouds or sun, rain or shine, feelings float by, fluttering up and down as they pass through their cycles of eternity.

*Wednesday, February 26, 2020*
*Patience*

I am fighting impatience. How to wait, dwell, in the relaxation spot (right wrist). Guitar, yoga, folk dancing, writing, all of them. Impatience is the fight against death. When you focus on patience, on the relaxation spot, you feel eternity and touch eternal life.

It stops time. Its positive benefit is the prize of peace.

*Friday, March 6, 2020*
*The End of a Dream*

Since college I've wanted to be a writer. And become a writer, and even define myself as writer.

During the intermittent fifty or so years I've still managed to write "on the side" while I earned a living in other fields.

Now however, especially this year, I'm at the point where we have enough money to "retire," even though, since we like our work, we never will. But this also means, at least mentally and attitudinally, that I am now finally free to write! In service of this view, I have finally started editing my work. And I see that, by careful editing, I could really be, become and, more important, call myself a professional writer. The door has finally opened. Paradise is at hand.

Except, now that I have limitless possibilities as a writer, suddenly, my writing limitations have opened up. I see that I can't write for more than an hour, maybe two at best, a day. I can't sit still and concentrate longer than that.

My idea of being a professional writer was that I'd be free to sit at my desk all day and write.

Maybe I've been living within my limitation all these past years but didn't realize it. After all, I have managed to write, and publish, many books. But as I say, always as a sideline, and as an "amateur."

Well, now I can. . . . But I can't. And these limitations are depressing me. It is depressing to realize that the chance to live my dream is really a nightmare in disguise. I have been fooled all these years. Unconsciously, subconsciously, unknowingly, all these years I have been fulfilling my dream as I live within my business restrictions and limitations. Where do I go from here?

## New Guitar Warm-Up: Awakening the Joy Juices

This is a new way of approaching the guitar. Instead of warming up slowly and carefully, jump right in to fast playing. But most important, with this approach, in order not to hurt myself, pull a tight cold muscle, start out fast and very light.

Light, even very light, playing is the key to non-injury and beginning "mentally" fast. In other words, the mind can begin, start off immediately in exhilaration mode. It takes a bit more time for the physical fingers and their muscles to catch up.

This is an opposite approach to the way I have warmed up, practiced, and played guitar all my life.

However, the old approach has never worked. My excitement, enthusiasm, and exhilaration have always been suppressed, nay drained out of my guitar playing, through the fear of making mistakes, not playing perfectly, being compared to the "pros" and master guitarists of the past. A fear-based approach has not been true for folk singing or folk dancing. Result: All my life, my self-image "believes" I cannot play classical guitar.

Perhaps this new approach, based on awakening exhilaration, excitement, enthusiasm, and joy, through the technique of speed, practicing and playing fast, will change things—and work.

## Monday, March 16, 2020
### Dealing with Worst-Case Scenario

Strange, but when I panic and despair, it doesn't really seem like me. Sure, I experience the miserable, down feelings and more. But when they end, I bounce up from the ocean bottom, and return to "someone else." Is that "someone else" the real me?

Joy, enthusiasm, art, and laughter seem like my real home. Am I right? I must deal with panic, despair, and depression, but they feel like detours.

Is my real home in Enthusiasm? After all, it means "In God."

## Wednesday, March 18, 2020
### Coronavirus Life

I broke down and cried last night. A sad crisis. Losing my business, my money, stock savings, future tours, and nothing I can do about it.

Well, I'm finished mourning. Time to move on.

To what? Many lessons from this Covid period. Perhaps most important, remembering (re-member-ing) how important people are. This obvious truth, often forgotten in ordinary times, is highlighted especially now in this isolation and social "distancing."

Yes, other people are so important. I miss them.

I am reminded of how all my activities aim at *other people*. That I expect to bring the fruits of my knowledge and talent to them.

What kind of life is there without people? Nothing. Death. Even monastic retreats, cenobitic or hermetic, are created for the purpose of self-healing, eventual re-entry, and helping others.

Social distancing may work as a short-term measure, but ultimately it can only fail. Without connection, everything loses meaning. Luckily, there is no death without resurrection. So I ask, when the world is lifted from this Coronavirus quarantine state, where will it be?

Using my creativity, I must imagine one beyond this Corona state. Where will I be in, say, two months? What am I aiming and practicing for? Can anything new come out of quarantine?

My answer is: Yes. I just don't know what it is yet.

### Exhilaration and Market Trading

Yesterday I spent all day trading stocks. My mind was totally free and focused to do it. It was the first day of my new stock market trading life. Yesterday turned out to be one of the best trading days I ever had. Much good and successful focus. Much money made. Excellent. Note: It was difficult to sit and focus on the screen all day. It exhausted and exhilarated me.

I must add movement to my new, before-the-screen stock market trading-focused sitting life, at least during the Coronavirus lock-down period.

Today's focus:

1. How to preserve my gains.
2. Maybe even move ahead a bit.

### Instinctual Survival: Panic as Smart

Do panic, and its hand-maiden terror, destroy confidence?

Or is panic a visceral form of smart? An instinctual animal survival skill, the "fight or flight" survival instinct?

By keying into panic, I am protecting myself, unleashing energy to save me to survive and thus fight another day. So instead of being ashamed, better is to be proud that I was smart enough to escape at the right time. In this sense, retreat is not defeat.

Of course, it was not a conscious, in-control decision to retreat but rather a panicked one, out of control, led by emotions rather than intellect.  But the result was the same.  I saved myself.  My animal instincts took over.

I cannot say fleeing is my finest moment.  On the other hand, why should I waste my brain being ashamed?  Better to see it as the revelation of a deeper animal self, the discovery of a new inner friend and protector.


### Levels Never End: Freedom

I cannot be free alone.  There is no such thing that can only be achieved through the imagination.  Freedom is achieved with *others*.  I'm not quite sure what that means, but I know it's true.

Would a hint of it be the "freedom and ecstasy" I feel leading folk dancers in a circle?  United with my group, we melt into one.  Isn't it the same as giving a concert?


### The Joy Finger

When I play guitar, what is the index finger expressing or blocking?  Could it be joy?  The joy finger, hidden and lost all these years.  Wouldn't that be great.  Bring joy to the world—now, that's something worthwhile!  That's a gift I'd definitely like to offer!


### Monday, April 20, 2020
### Coronavirus Lock Down

This morning I'm at the bottom, totally knotted in rage.  In frustration, I have turned my anger at the government on myself.  Those idiots have destroyed my business and taken away half our savings, along with my ability to work and earn a living.  I'm totally enraged, and have been so since this insane stupid shut down.  Now I've turned the fury of this energy on myself by twisting all my former purposes into a knot and shutting myself down.

The rage I feel toward my government at its utter timidity and stupidity for shutting down our entire society over a mere virus, this inner rage has, rather than bursting out in helpless frustration, turned its poison forces inward on me. Like a gigantic snake, the enraged tentacles have wrapped themselves around my energy and squeezed it out of me. I started sneezing this morning, and have a slight cold, and this over nothing. My resistance is low, actually squashed, and this because I feel squashed.

Is there anything better I can do with my anger? At the moment, I can't think of a thing. First the government tries to destroy me. I fight back. But now, my fury has worn me down, and I seem to be giving up. I feel helpless.

Seems self-destruction is the only route I want to take this morning. Well, at least I have control over it, and that's something. Since this is my present situation, maybe the best way to handle it is to self-destruct as far as I can go, and see where it leads.

On a more positive note, this destruction may also be tearing down the perfectionist classical guitar prison I have built for myself. If true, this is a destruction I would love.

## Tuesday, April 21, 2020
### Retired

Okay, as of today, I am "retired" by the situation. No job, no folk dance teaching, no tours. Even the lockdown supports the idea. Society itself has retired. Everything has stopped. I've stopped because all my businesses have stopped. Not a start to be found. Only, up to now, I have rejected this state by trying to "see beyond it," to the time when, one day, I will be "allowed" to work again. But that time is slipping further and further away.

So it occurred to me—why not think in a new way? Since I have been retired, isn't this a good time to "practice" retirement? In fact, why not take it a step further and believe it? Yes, I'll do that. Starting today, I *am* retired.

What does it feel like? What does it mean? First, all pressure to earn a living is gone. (True, I used to love this idea. I still do. Well, I can cry in remembrance, but nevertheless, it's over. It also reminds me that nothing can or will change except my attitude.) The second thing is that my guitar playing no longer matters. I no longer see myself playing before an audience. What does this do for my playing? I hope it helps free me to be imperfect, step out of self-imposed prison, and "play like the wind," the way I did yesterday.

In other words, this supposed state of "retirement" means possible freedom from the chains of perfection, the suffocating push-down of my inner critic, and pressure from others to do things their way. Not a bad start.

The stock market is crashing again today. I'll lose more money. How should I view this fact? I could choose the pessimistic view and panic. I just did.

But I could choose an optimistic view: It's a buying opportunity. I also realized I had the foresight to sell 300 shares of RST a few days ago, when the market was up. So I raised some cash. I could buy something today. Just nibbles, a small amount, maybe 50 shares of RST, and 25 of XOM.

Best to view a down market as a buying opportunity. Notice how this optimistic view raises my spirits and inspires me to act. It is so good for heart and mind. And, since we really never know the future, an optimistic view is a choice. I'll choose it simply because it's good for me. Then I want to learn the benefits of losing money in the market. How is the CV shut down good for me? Or how is losing my tour and folk dance business good for me? Any *benefits?*

This will take work, and lots of creative thinking. But if I can think of reasons to be hopeful, optimistic, and upbeat, such a positive attitude in crisis is simply better for my health. Find, create, invent, and choose it for that reason alone. And for the health of others as well.

Learn how margin works, and how it is measured. Part of my new job is to be more exact with numbers. Eventually, I'd like to take money out of the market, and even earn a living through it. Make some money. Do it right. Why? I hate a mess.

But is hating a mess enough to motivate me? Am I "serious" about my new stock trading "profession"? Is it a skill I really want? Or only a hobby, something to amuse myself with? Do I have any real love or interest in finance and money. Of course, there is fear, and the need for some security. And fear does create "interest." But it doesn't necessarily create love. And ultimately, once fear evaporates and I feel secure, all that will be left to motivate me is love.

## Sunday, April 26, 2020
### My Fatal Mistake

Why am I puzzled? What was my mistake? I put too much faith in government and leaders, and not enough in myself. Give up on them. Do that and I'll be happier! Put my confidence, faith, and power in myself. Move past these moronic lock-down Corona decisions of leaders and government. They won't be able to figure it out. I, along with regular, everyday folks, will. Our president, by listening and handing over his leadership to health professionals, has lost his way. That's why small government is good. The bigger the government, the bigger the mistakes.

## Tuesday, April 28, 2020
### A Wahoo Trading Day

I am blown away, thrown off kilter, by yesterday's successful day of stock market trading—basically, winning in such a way made me feel gloriously happy! Today, and immediately after my victory, I wanted to stay calm and collected. But I couldn't, and can't. Can I accept such joy? Me, a mere and formerly miserable trader? Can I now eliminate the word "former"? Can I even eliminate the word "miserable"?

Yes, I've made a commitment to trading, and yesterday it paid off. I succeeded. Can I proudly make this commitment part of my life? I want to be proud of myself, of the direction I've chosen, of my fighting and undefeated spirit, of my skill, and the fact that I lose some, win some, and still move on. I want my wife to be proud that I dare take chances, speculate, even lose in the learning process.

I doubt I can ever make her feel that. Just as we disagree politically, I think we will always disagree on my desire to take the adventure of stock market trading. Despite these disagreements, we love each other. Such is life.

*Saturday, May 2, 2020*
*Long Run Principle*

One thing about the long two-hour run I took yesterday is that, after an hour or so, your brain, along with your pain, shuts down and you start running "automatically" and somehow without pain. The muscles open up, relax, and loosen. You move on automatic.

Maybe the same thing will work with my guitar tremolo. Just play it like a long run, which means over and over again. "Alhambra" four, five, ten times, even more. As I do, the muscles "relax almost by themselves and start moving automatically. Soon the tremolo improves "by itself."

*Wednesday, May 6, 2020*
*Less Greed Equals Less Fear*

What did I learn today trading stocks? Take smaller "careful" steps. Smaller and careful equals less greed. Less greed equals less fear. And vice versa. Do I want less fear and greed? It means the size of my "thrills" go down. Do I want fewer thrills? Is that "better" for me? Maybe. Or maybe the balance will change from day to day.

Less greed and fear will make me wiser and better as a trader. Do I *want* to be wiser and better? Am I willing to give up the thrills of youth for the wisdom of old age? Maybe. Now that the choice has been revealed, do I even have a choice?

*Thursday, May 7, 2020*
*Smooth up Your Attitudes*

The Coronavirus lockdown has forced me into retirement. Last night we went over our finances and discovered we can do this. We can retire. Yes, and presently I am retired, or rather, have been. Whatever I want to call it, the fact is, and will continue to be for a while. that all my work has stopped. Do I like this retirement? Partly. Do I have a choice? No. Is this a hiatus, or permanent change? Too early to tell. . .but interesting.

Should I give up tours and folk dancing? Or use this hiatus to prepare for the next stage? (I estimate the hiatus will be about a year.) But now my purpose for working would be "beyond money." Or would it be? Maybe money is an "interest-in-itself." Is it a good-in-itself? For me, yes, since it motivates me. Okay, so maybe this period is "merely" a long break, which give me some free time and space. What will I do with it? How will I "prepare?"

*Friday, May 8, 2020*
*Love and Trading*

Start with love. I love trading. It's so much fun! How to keep it that way? Soften the fear and greed aspect. Start with taking smaller positions. This is hard to do. Why? It militates against the excitement of greed and the opposite excitement of fear. Greed and fear are the giant emotions of the stock market. Could the clash of greed and fear synthesize, and in the process, rise above themselves and create love? I'd like that. I do know that when greed and fear synthesize, they create calm. Calm creates perspective. Perspective can create love.

*Sunday, May 10, 2020*

It's fun making up dances, choreographing them in body, mind, and spirit. Why not choreograph with guitar, song, and writing? It is my form of play. The ability to play, and the joy it brings, are a contribution to the world. Remind myself to always play. And as I remind myself, it reminds others. A special gift. Thus, to really play it, choreographing, changing the music and expression along the way, I make it mine. Yes, the composer composed or choreographed it in his or her way. But I, as a per-form-er, re-choreograph it in my own way, and thus re-introduce the creative process to myself and my audience.

*Creating a New Guitar Self*

I am still in "Alhambra" prison and have been incarcerated there for years. I'll have to break down the walls, destroy the old "Alhambra" self, before I can escape and create a new, liberal "Alhambra." Perhaps my path to freedom and a new guitar self is to give up playing the "Alhambra" for weeks, months, years, or even forever.

Note: The Coronavirus has made me give up folk dance teaching and tours for weeks, months, maybe years, and even forever. In the process, it may create a new folk dance and tour self.

### Trading Fun and Joy: "Breaking" Out

My body feels broken this morning: lower back and leg pains, maybe accentuated by my long run yesterday. Could also be usual morning stuff. In any case, how to look at it? Differentiate between how I feel and how I actually am. I've felt this all before. Old stuff. I know it will all go away once I move around and exercise.

But I also want to believe that this morning's aches and pains symbolize a new beginning. What's new? Perhaps seeing myself as a competent trader. My morning pains have been created because my mind and body are "breaking" out of the panic and impending doom of existence, and expanding, pushing my goal of becoming a good trader. I'll only know and believe I've arrived when I make money. What a victory that would be. Since I want to believe it, maybe I should choose to. Do I really have such control of my thoughts and wishes? Yes. My wishes represent the future and are motivational thoughts in disguise.

By choosing my wishes, can I turn them into truth? My wish now is to make money as a trader. Start trying this morning when the market opens. Aim to fulfill my wish now.

### Saturday, May 16, 2020
### Cycles and Turning Points

It feels like a miracle. The times I truly give up are a turning point, the place where opposites are born. Nothing ever ends. I only imagine it does. My fears and limitations create the negative feelings. But they run their course, sliding downhill until they reach bottom, then turn around and heading upward. Round and round the cycle goes.

This is my first glimpse of gratitude, of thanking the virus for giving me a year off to think, change, grow, and develop.

Everything feels different. Maybe it's a good thing.

*Sunday, May 17, 2020*
*Folk Aerobics*

The benefits of Coronavirus are starting to stream in. This plague, descended from heaven to teach me new survival techniques, is now teaching me to live and even thrive with them. What has my teacher, Mr. Corona, taught me? What retirement feels like. I'm developing my stock trading skill, plus the new art of folk aerobics. (Folk dancing without holding hands does not create the same sense of community as when folk dancers hold hands. I don't know what to call it, but it is quite different.)

The Coronavirus lockdown is pushing me to develop a new, joy-based, non-hand-holding dance form. Although obviously not folk dancing in the traditional sense, it is nevertheless a new, solo, free-form art. I'd put it in the folk tradition of rugged American individualism and entrepreneurial invention. By its very nature, folk aerobics uses social distancing. But I'll need a new positive name for it. I'm beginning a home-made Eleusinian mystery cult, dancing with masks such Greek beauties as Dionysian Syrtos or Hasapico Soteriologiko.

*Master Chord of the Universe*

What is miracle guitar playing? I can't be God. But I can be His representative. I can bring His C chord to others. And myriad other chords as well. Within them are messages on living, dissertations on self-treatment, how to treat others, unify the atmosphere, and save the world. As His representative, I can bring the celestial notes to His audience. This C-elestial chord is not called the C chord for nothing. I'm playing the stately Milan "Pavane in C." Upbeat, majestic, proud, and royal, I welcome the All-Is-One King embracing the universe in His loving arms.

As I play the Milan "Pavane," I greet my audience with a splash burst pluck of C triad, sounding and spreading the master chord of the universe. Amazing that I dare. Am I worthy? Or will my lofty thoughts simply dribble away, be forgotten, and vanish into the morning mist?

What knowledge can be gained from this royal visit? Dare to amaze.

## Monday, May 18, 2020
### Miracle Day

Miracles are gifts from God. When they happen, it seems like they are bestowed by accident. Are they? I can hope for a miracle, but I can never expect one. Or can I? Maybe miracles are not as rare as I think. Maybe they're all around me, but I just don't see them.

If this is so, then it's more a question of opening my mind to the events that daily take place around me, accepting the daily miracle of life. Although miracles are a gift I can't create, it is within my power to see them. This means that by merely opening my eyes, I can add them to my daily life.

### Motivation and Promotion

The stock market is about making money. That's what makes it interesting. But what about selling my books? If it is no longer about making money, what will motivate me to promote them? Are they important? That would give me a good reason to promote them.

I'd need not only confidence in my books but also the belief that reading them will help others. I think so "Believe" is a shade better. "Certainly" is better yet. "Absolutely" is best.

## Tuesday, May 19, 2020
### The Pressure to Excel

My job is to imagine my future business and figure out what I will create for it. Am I a people person? I really don't see myself that way. I see myself as a loner, a soloist, a closet monk, an alone (but not lonely) musician playing solo violin in my teenage room. I love my time alone, to sit, stand, run, or play, enjoying my contemplations.

In fact, I never see myself as *with* people.  Oh, yes, I need them, but mostly as a source for food and emotional sustenance.  I don't remember ever "enjoying" people until I became a social director at Chaits Hotel in the Catskills.  I enjoyed "playing" with them, standing around with them, laying back on my heels, and having a riotous inner laugh as we bantered together. We all loved it and had a great time.  At least I did.

In fact, I see most of my inner life as trying to escape from people, from their influence and clutches, of trying to find and establish how to do things my way, beyond their influence and my need to please them.

Perhaps that's the key: *my need, even desire, to please them.*  How long have I had this hidden need?  Since I was born?  Or did it start later in life, after my teenage years?  Or after college?  Or was it always there, hidden in the darkness, submerged under my intense solo search for self?

Business and money have connected me to people.  And vice versa. My artistic side is the solo side, the part that wants to be alone, become a monk, slide into the corner and contemplate, create, imagine, and roll along.  Well, this Coronavirus period has removed the business, social director, advertising, and promoting side of me. Without the prospect of a future performance for others, I am also losing my motivation.

Evidently, my R and D must lead to a product or service, which I can then bring to the public.  It's a two-punch affair. Create, then deliver. Or create and deliver.  One is dead without the other.  On the artistic side, I need to create; and on the business side, I need to deliver. What happens when half this equation is lost, when the business side is cut off through solitary confinement?

Perhaps my job is to imagine working for my future public. Yet I hate performances.  But do I really?  Maybe I'm wrong.  Maybe Coronavirus is making me realize that I am only afraid of others and of the pressure to excel that they put on me.


*Wednesday, May 20, 2020*
*Paradox*

Do I want to put in the time and effort to learn Zoom?  Resistance to effort and love of effort are twins: You can't have one without the other. Should I learn Zoom even though I hate it? Hatred creates energy. Doing Zoom could push me into creating a new format that I love. What a paradox.

*Friday, May 22, 2020*
*Depression*

Is depression a choice? It doesn't feel like one, but maybe it is. If so, why do I choose it? Perhaps because it has some benefits. First, it takes no effort. I don't have to put in any energy. Like a pig in the mud, I can simply lie down to wallow in my oink-less, energy-less, depressive state.

Fighting off depression takes effort, energy, focus and concentration. And that's exactly what I don't want to give. I could fight it off if I really had something important I had to do. But I don't. So I'd rather not. My lazy self steps in and says, "Don't bother. I'll take over."

I sigh and say, "Oh, okay. Go for it, and give in.

So depression is really a choice. I choose inertia over dynamism, rest over action, listlessness over excitement, laziness over strength. I choose a resting place, enclosed and smelly, with an unpleasant odor of cesspool mist surrounded by heavy shadows, one that feels more like a coffin rolling on its way to Hades than the pleasant shade of a tree or warming sun on a Aegean beach. But at least it is a rest.

*Saturday, May 23, 2020*
*The Answer*

The struggle between freedom and slavery never ends. Freedom brings courage, inspiration, enthusiasm; slavery brings fear, depression, and stunted growth. The eternal fight between them in society reflects the human soul itself. Who will win? Today, with Coronavirus descending, slavery and fear are rising, their winnings displayed through the sour fruits of lock-downs, social distancing, and masks. Masks muzzle freedom, just as social distancing diminishes our connections. A sad state. Humans cannot exist too long with social distancing, masks, and the muzzling of social and productive instincts. How long can you live in slavery and fear? How long should you?

You can't live under lock-down. So first the lock-down will stop. Then, as people wander freely through their streets and fields, they'll have to decide whether, in their new-found freedom, they will choose to remain free, giving up social distancing and masks, accepting the risk of getting sick from the virus or any other disease, and thus live in freedom, with courage, inspiration, enthusiasm, fun, and joy, or go back to slavery and a life of fear, depression, sadness, misery, with zero growth and expansion. But no matter where they choose to live, whether in freedom land or the exile of slavery, the competition between the two world powers will go on forever.

It's called life. Like a chameleon, always changing its form, the struggle goes on. Some days freedom wins; other days slavery wins. Back and forth, over days and centuries, the eternal struggle rolls on. That's life, too. If the above is true, and it is, how shall I look at this Coronavirus time period? As an extended sabbatical, an R and D break, a welcome hiatus and vacation. My personal vaccine is hard R and D work! Yes, hard research and hard work opens the door to a new notion of what is possible!

## Sunday, May 24, 2020

My mind moves quickly from one mood to another. What is real? Does mood make reality? On a personal level, I'd say yes. But personal is only a small part of the picture. If my moods are so changeable, and my decisions so temporal, how can I trust or believe in my decisions? Maybe they're real and true but only for the moment. They could change the next moment as both reality and my mood change. They say life and reality are in the moment. All material reality is flowing.

Maybe these sudden mood changes are simply reflections of that reality.

That said, should I bother creating and offering private folk dance lessons on Zoom? After all, this Corona crisis may pass. And since I dislike teaching folk dancing on Zoom, and my offerings feel somewhat distasteful, why should I even bother doing it? Life is short, time is precious, and wasting it is basically stupid.

### Do What I Love

The months are passing quickly. I could be back to normal folk dancing and touring "before I know it." If time is so short and moving so fast, why bother with all these sideline folk dance distractions? Why not go with what I love.

Well, what do I love? Do I even remember? I've forgotten, and it's scary. What is my vision? The earthly realm of fear and worry tells me that time vanishes quickly. The heavenly realm of All-Is-One, eternity, and love tells me: Do what I love.

### Fight On

I dipped into the deepest depression. Inside me, everything collapsed, energy drained out, and I gave up. After three hours of the deepest downs, I realize why. First, I gave up on one of my great loves: classical guitar. After that, everything else collapsed. What is the moral of this story? Better to fight, even to the death. And note, this deathly down came the day after I found a new video purpose! I was so enthused about it yesterday! I wonder if it's part of the decision-making whipsaw. Well, now I'm back on track. I'll make classical guitar YouTube videos. Bad, dull, uninspired, it doesn't matter. I can always work to improve them. Better to end up with a miserable product and fight on.

Ultimately, giving up with its concomitant depression doesn't work. I'm tossed back into the ring to fight again. Once I get into the fight, it's not so bad. Actually, it's satisfying and fun!

### Tuesday, May 26, 2020
### The Gospel According to Gold

By focusing on service to others, I could forget about myself. That would be a wonderful thing. I'd remember my function, focus, and purpose: To bring joy, beauty, and even a bit of fun to people. To play my role as the divine fool. What a blessing to remember this purpose! "Fool" takes care of the fun and joy part, and beauty takes care of the divine. But are joy, beauty, and fun separate realms? No. They are one, the All-Is-One trinity. My purpose, for myself and others, is to spread joy, beauty, and a bit of fun through the world. There is no better gospel. And I have the skills to do it. My job is simply to remember this.

A challenging task! But nothing could be wiser. Every day the storms, pains, black clouds, sufferings, and foggy miseries in life push me into forgetfulness. Watch out for it! Thus, the gospel according to Gold.

# Re-Invention

# Picking Up The Pieces

*Monday, June 8, 2020*
*If One Person Loves Your Work, What Benefits!*

Why is it important that one person loves your art? Because if one person does, so could another. Two could double to four, four to eight. on and on until you have a huge following, a grand audience, your business flourishes, and soon you become rich and famous.

Not bad for a shy, retiring artist.

*Positive Benefits of Misery: Thank Your Depression*

Today time is running out. Death is up ahead. But today is no different from yesterday or any other day. So what's the big deal? Today I'm older. But I'm always older. I'm closer to the end. But it can end at any age. So why am I bothered by mortality today? It's just a slow day. But there is something I'm worried about.

It's the Wow Factor. Before I wrote this piece, I had a glorious idea. Start a *Dance of the Week* newsletter. An exciting new business rising from the Corona shut-down ashes. What a thought! Ideas flashed right and left. A wild, kabbalistic creative fire engulfed my being. I raced to my computer and dashed through my folk dance choreography videos, trying to decide which to choose. It got more intense as I struggled to organize the idea. Soon, I couldn't stand it anymore.

What better way to quell the flames of passion than hose it down with thoughts of impending doom, death, depression, and sundry other buckets of misery? Passion can be dangerous. In my state of invention ecstasy, I might believe I could fly. Then I might try it and jump off a cliff. Too excited was I. Luckily, I get depressed. It calms me, lowers my wild brain currents to a more stable place. The whack of sadness extinguishes the passion fire, protects me from emotional extremes. There are positive benefits from misery. It can relax me. Thank you, Depression.

### Start Writing Again

Totally retired by Coronavirus, I woke up with no goals in mind. No job, no outside force motivating me, no reason to get up or put effort into anything. Why bother getting up at all? Usually, this vacuum-packed, cosmic-depression state means I need to start writing again! In fact, just saying *writing* makes me feel better. Seems I'm on the cusp of writing fiction again. I'd also like to make some money. Selling my fiction would validate my writing efforts. Strangely, sales don't necessarily motivate me. But the feeling of cosmic emptiness does.

### Dissolving Internal Guitar Bullies

I have been pounded by internal classical guitar bullies most of my guitar-playing life. Notice I say "internal" because, truly, no one has insisted I play guitar in any other way but my own. The devils pursuing me for years are all creations of my imagination. These bullies had settled in "Recuerdos da la Alhambra" by the 19th century Spanish guitarist and composer Francisco Tarrega. This gorgeous tremolo piece became their stronghold, their castle lodgings for years. It has been my challenge to expel them.

But somehow Coronavirus infected them. They became weak, sick, and finally dissolved into a stream of dribble, floated out of the castle, passed through the gate, crossed the moat, and disappeared into the wild fields beyond. Now my castle feels clean and free.

Will these bullies return? I doubt it. Their chambers have been cleaned, polished, and sanctified. There is no longer a place for them here. Their defeat has been total. How and why this exit took place is a miracle, a gift of grace I may never understand. Of course, miracles are not for understanding. Perhaps it is a virgin birth. In any case, happy, naïve, and innocent, I can welcome in a new day.

*Saturday, June 13, 2020*
*Coronavirus Turning Point: Choose Life*

My choice is almost between life and death. Is it really "almost"? Or totally true? I'm afraid it's the latter. I hope it isn't, but maybe it is. Deep in my heart, I know it is the choice between freedom and death.

I hate this choice. But the Coronavirus political reaction, with its lock-down, destruction of the economy, destruction of my business, throttling of joy, love, and social contacts, mask muzzling and shutting off my freedom, social distancing with its killing of folk dancing, holding hands, touching, hugging, and flesh contact with real people is forcing me to make a life-and-death choice. And, of course, although it is awfully tough, and death is always an option, I still choose life.

*Sunday, June 14, 2020*
*Go with the Flow*

Although my Corona panic has diminished to a trickle, I'm still wasting lots of time in a rage about politics and the new social mores of masks, social distancing, riots, and protests. Truth is, I can't do anything to change things. Still I fume, turn the poison gases of panic and rage on myself, rail against these injustices, thought my anguish and mental energy seem ultimately to change nothing. This morning I'm giving up panic and anger. Accept things as they are and move on. It's in my control, possible, and easier.

*Wednesday, June 17, 2020*
*The Blessing of Losing My Business: A New Audience*

The belated benefits of Coronavirus shutdown are, among other things, a new audience of inner friends. My old audience was so critical, ready to pounce on every mistake, like hungry wolves waiting for the moment to jump on stage and tear me apart. My right hand froze playing every tremolo. But now, thanks to Covid and the destruction of my businesses, I have created a new inner audience, a select group of self-created friends, all sitting in a semicircle in our backyard.

My new concert program is performed for them. My classical guitar pieces, songs, and stories are now forms of meditation. Giving a concert has become a time for folks to sit, relaxed and happy, listening to music I create while their minds wander through the universe, visiting distant mystery centers to discover planets featuring love, beauty, and inner peace.

# The New Land

# Unfamiliar Terrain

*Tuesday, June 30, 2020*
*Stand Against Tyranny: Folk Dance!*

I'm not a politician. But I still need to fight their terrible decisions, which so negatively affect my life and the lives of others. The Coronavirus has locked out fun, excitement, joy, and growth, and replaced it with masks, social distancing, and shutdown misery.

Of course, public health is important. But without a functioning economy, everyone will die. Obviously, you need both. And for a civilized life, you also need sport, art, and adventure to enrich your garden. So the struggle to reopen begins. What's my best weapon? Folk dancing!

Open up folk dancing somewhere, somehow, even if, as a start, we must social distance and wear masks. Running dance classes puts the folk dance army on the march. Folk dance itself is its own subtle, powerful political statement. To win this battle, I need to open up my classes.

Dancing in parking lots and outdoor restaurants is a good start.

*Friday, July 3, 2020*
*Burden?*

My long run ended with left ankle pain. My first reaction was, Now I don't have to folk dance! Is teaching folk dancing a burden? I never thought of it that way, but maybe it is. The fact I must show up to teach, focus on my class, is a responsibility and thus a burden. A likeable, upbeat, pleasant, inspiring burden, but a burden nevertheless.

*Waiting for the Call*

I need a new source of motivation. One old source of motivation was fear. But most of it is gone now, replaced by rising confidence sprinkled with success. But somehow success has diminished motivation. What will ignite energy and inspire me toward uplift? Beauty? I see no other choice. Serving Beauty, bringing it to others, can be a calling. But is it enough to call *me?* Can it draw me out of the house and into the public square? I know my arts bring benefits to others. But is it enough to force my butt off the chair? So far, lethargy rules. Or is it paralysis? I'm stuck in mid-stream house, paddling forward and backward, waiting for the call.

### Wednesday, July 8, 2020
### Trading Victory

Yesterday's market fell 400 points. But I lost very little. This is good. Am I getting better? Or will I succumb to hubris? How did I succeed yesterday? First, I started out with two great penny stock wins. However, I sold them immediately and locked in my gains. (I didn't wait for them to go higher, as I used to. That's a learning plus.) Second, I have a new commitment: Do not lose money. This means I cut my losses early through tight stops. By softening my greed, I'm softening fear as well— by accepting lower gains, but also lower losses. So, by diminishing fear and greed, I ended up making money in yesterday's down market. I'll call this first victory over fear and greed. At least for a day.

### Sunday, July 19, 2020
### Monastery Life

I used to think retreat from the world was a good thing, but now I wonder. I admired my inner monk and the romantic desire to live in my inner monastery where art and imagination dwelt. But I wonder.

With Coronavirus dominating the world, I have mucho free time to dwell in my monastery. Since I lost all my business and reasons to promote and advertise in the outside world, my inner monastery has been fed to the point of satiation. . . and danger. I now face a lifetime question: How to deal with the material, outside, so-called real world. I need a balance between my socialized outer self and my inner, reflective, monastery self. I have added Dance of the Week website to bring me public. Another step toward going public.

## Reaching Out!

Start right away. With the first note, the first yogic stretch, the first weight, running, or dance step. Reach out!

The hypothenar area is the reach-out guitar spot. Expansion begins as soon as I pluck the first note. No warm-up needed. Reaching out *is* my warm up. Even when the body and muscles are cold.

## Thursday, July 23, 2020
## Guitar and Creative Chaos

One result of Corona retirement is playing the Milan "Pavane in C" with my right hand mostly over the sound hole.

Of the three sound color spots on the classic guitar, playing over the sound hole creates the sweetest sound. (Playing over the rosette is stronger, near the bridge more metallic.)

Retirement leads to soft, sweet guitar playing. No need to impress an audience, since retirement means I have no audience. Open to a new level of freedom, I happily step into the creative chaos.

## Thursday, July 23, 2020
## Leadership Life

Grab the leadership life! Leadership life emphasizes creativity, imagination, dynamism, social direction, performance, and uses imagination and creativity to change the world. Not a bad start. Dare to be bold. Get used to it.

## Friday, July 24, 2020
## Audience as Motivator and Energizer

As I was walking down Cedar Lane, I saw my refection in a store window. Slightly stooped as I walked slowly, I suddenly remembered my sister telling me to *walk correctly with long, strong, proud strides.* With her command in mind, I straightened my neck and proudly lengthened my stride. I felt better immediately! Why is this important? Because along with the good feeling came a vision of an inner audience watching me. It's the one I've been fighting with for years, trying to escape ever-critical eyes. But suddenly, as I took my grand, prideful stride, I no longer saw them as a repressive force, but rather as a great motivator and energizer!

Excitement shot to the surface. I straightened even more, with even greater pride. I walked straight ahead and I did it right! Why this happened today after so many years of inner struggle, I'll never know. But whatever the reason, I was ready.

### Tuesday, August 11, 2020
### The Art of the Mistake: A New Freedom Art Form

Let *The Art of the Mistake* take its rightful place among the performing arts. In aesthetics, clarity is a value. But is it a universal one or just mine? Moral judgements are based on the Ten Commandments; artistic/aesthetic judgements are based on personal tastes. For example, look at a Jackson Pollack painting, or read, if you can, James Joyce's *Finnegan's Wake*. Clarity is gone, destroyed, has no value at all. Yet some consider it art.

When I play or listen to classical music, clarity, the clear and perfected notes of the performing artist, are an important value. But again, look at atonal "modern" music. (Schoenberg and beyond): unorganized, chaotic, garbled, and proud.

So on my endless search for personal and artistic freedom, I ask: Could my sloppy playing of "Alhambra" still be considered art? (Of course, "sloppy" is my own term. I could call it something else. Gray? Indefinite? I see it as lack of skill. But that could simply be my own way of seeing it.)

My interpretation could change, I could see it as my own form of Jackson Pollack or *Finnegan's Wake*, my own addition to the new, postmodern art of "garbling" In other words, is there, could there ever be a hallowed place for mistakes in classical music? And if not, can I make one up?

Why not? Invention is my bag. Why not create a new space for creative rationalizations that turn mistakes into art. There's the *Art of the Deal*. Why not The *Art of the Mistake?* On one level, this seems like a joke. However, the unconscious works in mysterious ways. Many new discoveries and directions begin as jokes.

*Wednesday, August 26, 2020*
*Love of Study Leaf*

I'm drifting into a study of ancient Greece. It feels so different. I'm no longer studying for my survival, no longer desperate to learn as much as possible so I can lead my tours to these foreign lands. I feel no pressure to learn or know everything. Only the fun, love, and joy of study.

*Guitar Flying*

Once your guitar technique is established, you just warm up, relax, and let your fingers fly. And once you're warmed up and the blood starts to flow, they fly almost by themselves.

*Friday, August 28, 2020*

There's the God spot and Devil's spot. Man fluctuates between the two. How to get from one to another? A great mystery. Could it be the resurrection spot?

# Strength

*Saturday, August 29, 2020*
*Zoom*

Should I teach folk dancing on Zoom to make my dancers happy? Is their happiness enough motivation? I hate Zoom. Dancing on it is no fun for me. No real people to hold, touch, dance with, no human sweat, wild energy, pungent odors, or vibrant smiles. Nothing. I love, want, and need to dance. But I'll need a good reason to do it on Zoom. Since I can't find one inside myself, can I find it outside? Maybe in the shine of their exuberant faces or the 11/16 kopanica rhythms pumping through their ethnic dancing hearts? After all, it's quite pleasant sailing down the Danube to a Balkan beat. Could I ever do it on Zoom? Is fulling *their* needs enough to push *me* over the artistic top?

What makes my dancers happy? Socializing with each other, holding hands, dancing in a circle, seeing the flesh of human beings—not on a screen, but right before their eyes! Zoom can't offer this. But in-person dancing can.

*Monday, August 31, 2020*
*Benefits of Long-Term Guitar Practice*

Fast, fiery, dynamic guitar playing. As I practice, fear of back sliding fades away. Such ancient playing will be a memory. Finally, even the memory will disappear. All good. As my playing changes, my self-concept changes. And if I can do it with guitar, why not with everything else? Experts say your body stiffens as you get older. But they could be wrong. Suppose instead of getting worse with age, your body gets better! It's happening with my guitar-playing hands. They are getting better. Why not the rest of my body? Maybe the experts are wrong, and I am right! Truth is, I am the only one who knows myself.

Truth flashes in my guitar-playing hands. Best to decide I am the truth. But I fear it. With it comes fear of my confidence, fear of the unknown, fear of new paths, fear of my power. But isn't life about conquering fears?

## Banned Is Beautiful

My stock jumped. A happy surprise. I got something for nothing. The hope for happy surprises is why I trade stocks. But somehow trading stocks, also called "gambling in the stock market," feels unhealthy, dark, and evil. That may be why it's attractive. I'm attracted to light, but also to darkness. I like to try new things, often in secret. No criticism when it's secret. It also feels vaguely evil, wrong, banned, bordering on criminal, but also exciting. Do banned and beautiful go together?

Banned *is* beautiful. This speaks to the dialectics of life, how opposites attract, fuse, synthesize, and create something new.

## Thursday, September 10, 2020
## Zoom

Watched Lee Otterholt's Zoom folk dance class. He's such a good teacher. I tremble to admit it, but maybe I'm ready to enter the Zoom world. I'm in a different place now. Watching Lee, and his excellent presentation—he has even improved!—I realized Zoom can be its own art form. Certainly it is in his hands. (Or feet.) Why not in mine?

Two questions: First, why have I avoided Zoom up to now? Too angry, furious, and panicked with the political lock-down, social distance, and masking reactions to the virus, and its shutting down of all my business, I went into a two-month melt-down. This, of course, included losing the beauty of folk dancing with others, seeing, holding hands, and touching live humans beings. All gone. I was, and remain, furious.

However, my fury and panic have softened over the months. I have also finished the hermit projects I gave myself to accomplish during these shut down months. When September arrived, a fresh breeze blew my way, saying, "I'm ready to go back to work!" But I have no work. No folk dance teaching, folk dance tours. No nothing. Therefore, I have to create work. I'm ready to do it.

That's step one.

Second, when I started my Outdoor Folk Dance program last Sunday in Teaneck's Fairleigh Dickinson University parking lot, I brought a strong speaker, checked everything out, and ran the class. Big success. Everyone loved it. I'll do more. Outdoor classes for Wednesday and alternate Sundays are now scheduled through November. After that, we'll see. I wanted to learn Busuiocul, so I asked Lee if he knew it. He said the best way to learn the styling is to watch his Zoom class. Which I did. Since I am in a new mental place, I watched it with new eyes. I also conferred with myself. "Why am I still avoiding Zoom? Is it cowardice, laziness, hatred, or something else?" Well, my Zoom hatred, with its sister, panic, has diminished to the point of disappearance. Then comes laziness, which I don't believe in anyway. Finally, I arrived at cowardice. And yes, I have to admit it, my avoidance of Zoom is partly due to cowardice: the hesitation and resistance toward trying something new. I can't live with cowardice. This means I have to take Zoom by the horns, wrestle it, and dive into all the glories and headaches that come with learning to use it. I'm trembling with hesitation, glory, disgust, excitement, annoyance, and all the stops and starts that come with a new project.

*Sunday, September 13, 2020*
*Sales and Promotion*

Where did the arrogance of "not needing others" come from? First thing that comes to mind is "being an artist." A true artist lives alone, stands alone, is impervious to the demands and desires of others, of the audience (the political masses) to please them. He is above them, a tower of strength in his isolation and the independence of his artistic vision. A true artist does not need to sell. He rises above self-promotion. Let the manager do it. That's what "they" are for. The pure artist stays in his ivory tower, unsullied by promotions and sales of self and his artistic vision. Such disdain and contempt for the public, the audience, the others! Softer for my "clients and customers." But that is since I got into business.

How did I arrive a such nonsense? I'm not sure. In any case, this Corona isolation has totally cleansed my mind of such poisonous, disastrous, destructive, and untrue notions. The river of nonsense has run its course. I need and love my audience. I am totally bound to others. Selling, and promoting, to them invigorate and energize me. Making money through them is the grand symbol of connection. Without them I am an isolated turd; with them, a shining symbol of strength, defiance, and hope.

I found two tour registrations in my emails, after six months of isolation. A miracle! Suddenly, I feel alive and hopeful. My tours and my future are back. I felt the same thing after I led our Parking Lot folk dancing last Sunday. I have something to sell and promote again.

Conclusion: I need and love to sell and promote things. It is a visceral need that invigorates, energizes, and inspires me, giving me a future that pushes me toward the light. Yes, I need to sell to customers. They, and the sunny sales process, are my energy source. I need to teach folk dancing, organize and lead my tours, promote my books, and give concerts. Monastic isolation and meditative aloneness are the inner engine. But the outward direction of sales makes the car roll. I need both. I'm a both kind of guy.

## Wednesday, September 16, 2020
### Resurrection of My Dreams

I fear old age, death, and the daily vulnerability of demise. Of course, added to this is losing all my business through the idiotic decisions of our political leaders. Not only has it caused me to give up hope, but also to cancel my dreams, and with that, the process of dreaming itself. My former dynamic dream state has been replaced by "Why bother? I'll be dead soon anyway." Is this a positive attitude? Is it realistic? Maybe. But this so-called realism is short-sighted, and its lack of vision makes it unrealistic. I like this line of thinking.

Realistically, I can replace these negative thoughts. So do it. After all, upbeat is better for your mental, physical, and spiritual health. Maybe my former so-called "realistic" attitude is really an illusion, a poison pill disguise for depression. Since this kind of depression is really anger turned inward, I now believe I'm just angry. If I stop and look deep in my heart, it's true: Yes, I'm mad as hell!

I'm furious at all the idiot politicians for closing down the economy, and destroying my business. As for my old age concerns, every age has problems. So deal with it and move on. Besides, old age is a secondary annoyance. Primarily, I'm enraged over the Coronavirus lock-downs.

What's the best fighting medicine, the best way to defeat my enemies? Form new shining goals. Resurrect my dreams. That'll show 'em! And show me, too.

### A Heavenly Start

I'm renaming my Milan's "Pavane in C" the "Resurrection of My Dreams Pavane." From now on it will be my opening concert number, my hello to the world. How uplifting are its majestic opening major chords! I'll think and play them that way. Thus, I'll start out immediately with a great message of optimism and hope. For my audience and myself. A gospel of resurrection in the first C chord!

### Saturday, September 19, 2020
### A New Look at The Index Finger

Focus on my index finger helps focus my mind on my playing rather than on the audience. It brings me inward. I feel its flesh against the string. Digital muscles and wrist relax. Soon my fingers align correctly, my body eases into the guitar. Mental focus follows. It is quite lovely.

### Sunday, September 20, 2020
### Glory of God

Bach composed his music for the glory of God.
I like that.

## The Path of Salvation

You work at something for years and nothing happens. You keep working for more years. . .still nothing happens. More years. . . . You can't rush the process. All you can do is practice, work, stay on the path. And one day it simply happens.

The moral: Keep working. Your power is the power of choice. You can choose to stay on the path. The path leads to salvation. But when and whether you arrive are not up to you.

## What Will the New Jim Look Like?

I'm forgetting the old life. Who am I? Who was I? Did I actually teach folk dancing? What about tours? Did I really lead them, organize and run them? Do I still play guitar? I find my definition and meaning floating away. Even the stock market and money worries are fading, dropping into the bin of ancient times. My guitar playing this morning started with a dizziness, a cramp in my neck, and a vague feeling of superiority. From there I moved on to playing confidently, with a feeling of ease, no worries, even a touch of greatness. Even though my body and fingers were cold, my opening "warm-up" "Pavane in C" felt effortless, a breeze. From there I played the Fernando Sor "Study in A." Again, easy, medium speed, somewhat effortless, a breeze. Then "Alhambra" with new confidence.

Forgetting some things is good. I'd love to forget my old inferior guitar-playing attitude, fears of no money, and lots of other confidence busters.

What do I want the new Jim to look like?

1. He plays guitar well.

2. He has few to no fears about money.

3. He is motivated to perform his professional and private tasks for the glory of God.

4. He walks like a dancer, runs like a dancer, and lives like a dancer, with the glory of God ever in mind.

5. He practices physical and mental balance

Yes, the Coronavirus agent of forgetfulness has wiped my slate clean. I am open and ready. Will my mind stay fresh and new? Will this cleansing last? Stay tuned.

## Monday, September 21, 2020
### The Bible Promotes Fun

The bible says David worshipped God by dancing before Him *v'simcha* (with joy). Worshipping with joy is the way to go. A goal of adulthood is see things fresh and new. Think like a child again. In other words, have fun. A worshipful and worthy goal.

### Soft

Playing guitar softly seems radical. It means taking a new look at masculinity and power. Where does power reside? Can it be found in soft? Yes. Play guitar softly, very softly. Forget about the audience. Forget about everything except the music, sound, relaxation, and touch. Let the healing power of letting loose cure invisibility. Soft is vibrational energy discovered in yielding, power through hidden power. Revelations are revealed through the hidden quiet shine of the sun within.

## Tuesday, September 22, 2020
### What's the Big Deal?

Why did I get sick? Why this miserable cold? Sure, perhaps I overdid the long hike with Ben two days ago, then again yesterday for two more hours. But I sense it's more than that. I relate it to my worry about my teaching at the opening of our first Wednesday outdoor folk dance class.

Somehow, I have, once again, worked myself into a grand tremble of pre-performance anxiety, and the attempt to deny my fears is creating a cold as a distraction. Easier for my brain to focus on sneezing and a stuffy nose rather than the nervousness that my upcoming teaching creates.

But now that I know my emotions, I can approach them with a different attitude. After all, I'm in a new post-Corona mental place. For example, I can see my outdoor folk dance class as an experiment and approach it with an attitude of curiosity. See if it works. This is a good approach, a positive attitude toward everything I do.

But so far, knowing this does not make the jitters disappear. Plus, after almost a lifetime of performances, I am still nervous when a new one comes up. Pre-performance anxiety is still the poison weed in my garden. No matter how much I try to "cure" myself, I never do. This bugger has never left me. Maybe the simple fact is: I will always be nervous before giving a show. It will never go away. I'll always be tense, on edge, or worse before any performance, whether it is a concert, leading a tour, or teaching a folk dance class. That's just my personality, the way I was made, the way I am. Such is life. Isn't it time I finally accepted this? Maybe my resistance, cowardice, lack of manliness, and inability to face my weakness are what made me sick in the first place.

On the other hand, maybe there's another way of looking at it. Could my weakness be my strength? Maybe, instead of weakening me, my anxiety wakes me up, gives me strength, energy, and power.

After all, look at what I accomplish. Plus, I never give in to my fears, I just tremble in place and move on to do the job. And it's usually an excellent job! After it's over people are happy, and I am happy. What could be bad about that? Only my unpleasant pre-action feelings. Otherwise, all is good. So what's the big deal?

*Saturday, September 26, 2020*
*New Guitar Warm-up*

When I play guitar I warm up immediately. I sit down, cradle it in classical guitar position, put my foot on the footstool and focus my mind focuses on the feel of the strings. Then I place my fingers in the C chord position for the opening chord of Milan's "Pavane in C." I touch the strings, feel them underneath each finger, pluck the strings, then listen to the tone I create. It's a four-step process: Touch, feel, pluck, listen. And voilá, after that process, I am warmed up, ready, and rolling.

## *Sunday, September 27, 2020*
## *The Wild Illumination of Writing Fiction*

I need to jump-start my brain with my own kind of fiction, my short-pieces writing style, with its outlandish humor, an inheritance passed down to me from my father, lifts my spirits.

Creating off-the-wall stories raises me up, brings me to another planet, flies me to a crazy, beyond-boundaries world of wild illuminations. As the protective shield against noxious incursions from the outside world, it frees my soul by placing it high above this sad, problematic life.

## *Saturday, February 13, 2021*
## *Strength Stock Trading*

How could strength show up in my stock market day trading? Rather than worrying I'll lose money, be wiped out, become a pauper, go to zero, let me give up my habitual doomsday scenario. Instead try: "I'll make money today!" Blow the clouds away. Clear the sky. Let the sun shine. Replace my "I'll lose money" black cloud with the clear skies of "I'll make money." See what happens.

## *Saturday, October 3, 2020*
## *Blessings of Uncertainty*

Uncertainty is uncomfortable. It creates bad dreams, sometimes nightmares. But uncertainty has a plus side. It forces you to pay attention, make greater effort. It increases your energy. Where will we folk dance? In which parking lot? This uncertainty, along with the uncertainty over whether the police will shut us down, forces me to think creatively. My jumbled, confused state is a perfect symbol of life. It builds intimate survival knowledge, opening the door to bending, twisting, and other techniques of flexibility.

I'm now ready to hold classes in any available parking lot, field, or street. The perpetual wanderer approach to folk dancing.

*Wednesday, October 7, 2020*
*Folk Dance Parking Lot Victories*

Last Wednesday the Fairleigh Dickinson University police said we had to get permission from the university to folk dance in their parking lot. I emailed the provost. Thursday I got an email: No rentals due to Coronavirus. Permission denied. Friday morning I went to the FDU security department, where I called the head of security to beg to dance in their parking lot at least for this Sunday. He said no. I came home, spent the rest of the morning looking for parking lots around Teaneck, and found a few public ones that might be free.

Then I called Lowell School and asked the assistant principal if we could dance in their parking lot. She said no problem, but soon called back to say she had done more research and that I needed to get permission from the Teaneck Board of Education. I called them. They said no. Permission denied again due to Coronavirus.

That's when I decided: No more asking. I'll just do it. From now on, we'll just dance in whatever parking lot we like. If the police come to throw us out, we'll just apologize, say we didn't know you had to ask for permission, and move on to the next parking lot. Just do it. If caught and stopped, apologize and move on to the next lot. We have now become the bandit folk dancers, breaking the rules, even laws, all for a good cause. Robin Hood would be proud.

Result: We had a wonderful illegal folk dance last Sunday in the Lowell School parking lot. A final technical problem occurred when my computer ran out of battery power and the music stopped in the middle of a dance. (Battery power is a recurring problem in parking lot folk dancing.) But I solved it with the help of my computer guru, Frank, who told me how to get electrical power by connecting to my car battery through the cigarette lighter! I bought an extension cord at Home Depot, and am now totally ready to roll. Parking Lot Folk Dancing, here we come!

*Tuesday, October 20, 2020*
*Power of Attitude*

Since attitude is created in imagination, why not imagine I'll live forever? Not only does this thought feel good, it could even be true. All religions agree eternal life exists. Why not believe it? It can only do me good.

### The Covid-Induced Coma of Freedom

When I play guitar with the Lord listening, understanding each tone. there's no pressure. Playing in complete freedom, luxuriating in each tone, I fly through the universe.

I've lost my rusty anchors and old boundaries. Perhaps I'm ready for the monastery. Just sit there in my Teaneck cell, or high up on a distant Syrian stylite monastic pillar, and play for God.

This Covid-induced coma of freedom feels strange, different, new. Somewhat sad, listless, weighed down, but also rich, heavy with transcendent purpose, welded to the earth while anchored in heaven. Perhaps the months of Covid lock-downs, social distancing, masks, and solitude have been a preparation for flying through the inner and outer space of freedom.

# Victory and Glory

*Sunday, October 18, 2020*
*Success*

I finally got it right.

The electrical supply from my car was in order, and the hood I created out of a carton covered the computer well, enabling me to see the screen in the sun.

I could program the folk dance class as it went along, creating new moods.

Finally, after many weeks of trying, all seemed in order. Victory at last!

I also wrote a successful article on outdoor folk dancing, and have a new MIT folk dance program from Murray to study and learn. Plus, thanks to Dan, a possible new self-definition as a self-help guru which is the key to promoting my New Leaf Journal.

And since I started taking smaller positions, my stock trading has become more peaceful and controlled. New directions are falling into place.

*Monday, October 19, 2020*
*Folk Dancing and Freedom*

Social distancing has destroyed holding hands in the folk dance circle. But it has also freed the folk dancers from certain restrictions. Freedom is good. But too much freedom leads to anarchy and chaos. That's not good. On the other hand, too little freedom leads to slavery. A balanced middle way, the golden mean, is the way to go. Freedom with discipline is best. To paraphrase Jean-Paul Sartre: The free man is one who can choose his form of slavery.

*Wednesday, October 21, 2020*
*Expanding Performance Mode*

I get a shot of meaning when I do things with or for others. For example, my parking lot folk dance class has energized me, awakened me from my Covid lock-down anger-panic-sadness-depression stupor. I'm up and ready to roll. This "with-others" stuff scares me a bit. I'm nervous before each class. But the wake-up power of purpose, the adrenaline rush that comes with the fear of criticism, and the idea that I stand before others with the possibility of total humiliation if I make a mistake or mess up, and the wonder and glory that come with success when my people love it, all this is my powerful jump-into-the-world stimulant.

*Sunday, October 25, 2020*
*Adding "Fiction Raw" to My Website!*

Now I know why every morning, since the beginning of the Corona shut-down, I've woken up with either panic, depression, or a headache. I've also stopped writing fiction. I ask, What's the big deal? I'm still writing daily in my journal. The answer is: I write in my journal to discover and explain myself to myself. It helps clarify the day. It is my vital form of self help, like eating basic foods in order to survive. Survival is an important ingredient in success. However, once you succeed, is there more to life than mere survival? The answer is, of course, yes. Writing fiction!

That's where great leaps of enthusiasm, sparks of happiness, bursts of celestial magnificence, come from. I can't beat writing an off-the-wall story to make my day. When these crazy ideas pop in my mind, then sprawl themselves across the paper, they make me laugh and cry in unadulterated joy. Puzzling, uninvited. and unexplained, I gasp and giggle in awe and wonder. Where did this come from? How did it happen? I have no answer. Nor do I care what it is, or if there is one. I am simply grateful that, through this mysterious process, I have been freed of ego and momentarily liberated to soar, wild and unencumbered.

These crazy stories are partly inherited from my father. He had crazy stories to tell us kids. So thank you, Pop! And this morning, I'm ready to take the plunge again into the mysterious waters of the Wild River. But before I leap, one more question: Anything else missing in my fiction life? Yes. Publication and recognition. A schizophrenic split between this obligation to promote and sell my books, and the desire to simply create them alone in monastic splendor, ever haunts me. But this morning I have a possible answer! I'll add a "Fiction in the Raw" section to my website.

This would solve the publication problem. It will also dispel most of my resentment toward sales and publishing. Just as President Trump uses Twitter to bypass the media, I can bypass the publishing houses by uploading my stories on my website. On my website, I can publish whatever and whenever I want.

I don't even have to concern myself with negative feedback or bad reviews. Since I put my *New Leaf Journal* on the site, no one has read it! Turns out it's much harder to get readers than I thought. For now, that's fine with me. I'd rather experiment on virgin fields empty of critics rather than go into battle right away. This way I'll build up my confidence for future falls that may occur, if I ever do get read.

*Friday, October 30, 2020*
*Feelings and Reality*

I feel much better this morning. I don't know why that doesn't matter. I love it just the same. Like clouds, feelings float through the sky, passing in and out, changing day to day, moment to moment, they always feel totally real. On one level, they are. But they always pass on, blown away by time itself, to be replaced by the next cloud, the next feeling, which again feels totally real. But if reality is measured by permanence, how "real" could feelings be? Transient, ever changing, floating clouds, wisps of illusion passing themselves off as reality itself, how real is that?

What can I do about this situation? Not much. . . there is one thing: Dive into them, get to know them, and, in the process, realize my feelings, although powerful, are but passing illusions. Awareness of that is all I can "do" about them. And it's enough—but it often takes strength, wisdom, and courage to do it.

*Tuesday, November 3, 2020*
*All-Is-One*

Is it true that All-Is-One? Yes. Whether I like it or not, I am connected to others always and forever. Happy or sad, that's the way it is. There is no escape. Every activity is either directly or indirectly connected to others. And this is true whether these "others" exist in the past, present, or future. Witness my new interest in biblical Greek. This is a dead language. But is it? It was once spoken by humans. I am interested in humans. I belong to this group. My interest in the ancient language of past humans therefore connects me to these ancients.

My work, social functions, family, and daily activities in the present are also all connected to others. My concerns about the future, how I will touch others in life or leave them through death, also connects me to them. (Is life permanent or temporary? Is death real or an illusion? We'll deal with these questions, and rebirth, resurrection, and reincarnation, another time.)

Summarizing: I am gloriously or miserably connected to others forever. Is this good or bad? These questions are really beside the point. From cradle to nursing home, womb to graveyard, connection to others is an eternal and infinite reality.

### Eternal Communication

By studying biblical Greek and Hebrew I am communicating with people in the past. By teaching folk dancing, running tours, doing business, I'm communicating with those in the present. By wondering about my direction and purpose, what will happen to me in life, I'm communicating with people of the future. People are forever. That's just the way it is.

### The Reality of Imaginary Audiences

The guitar concert I am practicing for will always have an imaginary audience, whether I give it public or not. Imagination creates reality. Is my imaginary audience real? Yes. As real as the biblical Greek-speaking audience that inspires me to learn biblical Greek. As real as tomorrow's folk dance class that inspires me to prepare a new program, introduce new dances, and bring back some oldies. Imaginary audiences are my great motivators.

## Wednesday, November 4, 2020
## We Are One

Everything I do is connected to others—even the things I do alone, which is most things. I study alone, practice guitar alone, go over my dances alone, exercise alone, I answer emails alone, prepare tour itineraries alone, write letters alone. But for all the time and effort spent alone, ever hovering in the back of my mind are the invisible others. And ultimately it is for them that I work. And play, too.

## Editing My Journal

Are reality and fiction separate? Are my fiction and reality? Since "perhaps" is my energy connection, perhaps reality and fiction are really one. If this is so—and I think it is—this could be the first step towards a desire to edit my journal. I have no trouble editing my fiction. But until now, editing my *New Leaf Journal* has been unimaginable.

## Friday, November 6, 2020
## The Tyranny of "Right" Pronunciation

I suffer from the tyranny of "right" pronunciation. I'm studying Hebrew and biblical Greek. What is the "right" pronunciation and how important is it? I know there are different pronunciations of languages throughout the world, and that, in different regions, people pronounce the same language differently.

I know the most important thing about pronunciation is understanding each other. I also know, since people pronounce the language differently throughout the world, that there are many "right" ways to speak.

Given this truth, why do I suffer from the tyranny of right pronunciation? Probably because I like to get things right.

But what is "right"? In my heart and soul, I still want to speak the correct way. And the correct way is, I think, believe, guess, is the way people pronounce the words in their native country. The right way to pronounce Hebrew is the way Israelis do it in Israel, the right way to pronounce Greek is the way the Greeks do it in Greece, etc.

But what about a so-called "dead" language like biblical Hebrew and Greek, classical Latin, Hittite, and Egyptian hieroglyphics? How do you pronounce the cuneiform writing of ancient Babylonian Code of Hammurabi? And really, what's the difference how I pronounce a dead language? Not many ancients to communicate with these days. Unless, of course, I use the present "accepted" pronunciation, so I can speak the dead languages to my contemporaries.

Lots of questions. But for me personally, it is simply a decision I have to make alone. After all, I am the one suffering from the tyranny of right pronunciation, so only I can free myself from these intellectual chains. I can start removing them by stepping out of my self-created prison, walking out and "pronouncing" myself a free man.

*Saturday, November 7, 2020*
*Going Slower: Jumping into the Fire*

The advantage of going slower is you go deeper. When I told this to David, he liked it. His appreciation of the idea confirmed its importance. Slow and fast have different purposes. Fast covers lots of distance and surface. Slow covers less but goes deeper. Both have their place in the pantheon of burning opposites. Opposites unite the cosmos. When slow and fast meet in the fire, they melt into One.

*Money as a Grand Motivator*

Money is a grand motivator. This is true whether I have lots or little. Consider my outdoor folk dance classes. I only ask for a $5.00 donation. After each class, I add up the small amount I receive. I wonder whether it's financially worth the effort of running the class. Then I feel the money, smell its greenness, sense the power in it, and, as it sits happily in my hands, I say, "Yes, it's worth it!" Money is a grand motivator.

Since this is true, can I use this green motivation to encourage me to promote my books? One way is to upload my stories and *New Leaf Journal* entries to my blog post.

This would serve the purpose of advertising my books and motivate me to edit my new writing. It would also give me an audience. I need one to motivate me.

### Sunday, November 8, 2020
### Defeat and Fighting Back

Yesterday I lost. But am I defeated? What's the difference between the two? Losing can happen anytime. You have little control over it. Defeated means you've decided to give up. Losing is an "outside" event. Defeat is an "inside" event, a thought, an attitude. As a teenager, I was a passionate baseball fan, rooting for, first, the winning Yankees, and then the losing St. Louis Browns. My emotions went up and down with their wins and losses. I also played baseball. In politics, I am a fan as well. But unlike baseball, I don't play politics. I am merely a fan. Note the word "merely." Like baseball, are politics for me *merely* entertainment? By using that word, I am diminishing the importance of this entertainment? Yes. Like baseball, I am hurt by the losses of my favorite team. Losing hurts. Period. Might as well admit it, deal with it, let the sadness and anger roll, and see where it leads. Finally, when the waves subside, move on. After a loss, the choice is to give up or fight back. It's healthiest for my psyche to fight back.

But how? Although I am a supporter, I really "do" nothing beyond being a fan. I join no parties. I spend no time promoting my political team. I simply watch from the sidelines and cheer. And I vote. That's all I want to do. Is just giving positive energy enough? Maybe.

On the other hand, maybe I am already in politics, doing it my own way, but just don't know or recognize it. Maybe my political way is the way of art, my personal apolitical political method.

After all, I do want to make the Earth a better place. I believe in *tik-kun olam,* healing the world. But my methods are different from the direct, in-your-face, hit-'em-over-the-head, bash-them-into-submission political methods of some others. Although I may share their philosophy and support leaders who do it this way, my method of subtle telepathic communication works.

I believe that, although on the surface, all people may not seem united, they nevertheless are.

All is One. I have my own method of bringing folks together. I use folk dancing, concerts, tours, my artistic method. When I work, I constantly think unity. That's how I unite my audience, or my students when I teach folk dancing, my tourists when I lead a tour.

Although my method is apolitical, in reality, it has big political meaning.

Maybe I'll create the first Folk Dance Party and make myself president. Of course, this is a joke. But maybe it's not as funny as I thought. Our party philosophy will be: We go in all directions, accept all people, and unify everyone through folk dance.

*Monday, November 9, 2020*
*The Truth of Slow*

Does going slow really open up a new world? I hope so. In this case, deep down "hope so" means know so. I know it's true. But I don't have the confidence to admit it yet. Also there is the fear that, by knowing, I'll kill, not only the hope, but the fact, truth, and reality of slow itself. If I jump immediately into believing my instincts, is it over confidence? Am I rushing the process and, in so doing, diminishing or even destroying it? In any case, the idea and practice of going slow opens up a new world. Is there a great truth in the slow process? Can it uncover great truths about myself and the world?

Deep down, I know it can. It already has. Example: Once I got past my shame of running slowly, I began to feel a new power in my legs. I'd have to call it the "power of slow." I'm amazed that I'm even saying this—but I am. For me, the shame of slow was blocking the power and wisdom of aging.

Shame is merely fear of judgment by others. A big "merely," but merely nevertheless. So shame boils down to fear. And fear, although it can block entrances and exits, is also an excellent motivator. Its best use is to inspire you to start doing what you're afraid of.

The physical fact is: I am entering a new stage. I am moving more slowly. New doors are opening. Slow is an important technique to use on the road to wisdom. And it ripens, gets better with age. Do I want to walk the slow road? Where will this lead? Do I even have a choice?

## Love Your Opposition

What can you do about the opposition? Basically, nothing. They will always be there. Opposition is a fact of life. The only control you have over them is your own attitude.

What's the best attitude? *Loving* your opposition is best. They stretch your mind, help you grow, teach you about weakness and strength. In the cosmic design, opposites attract and need each other. Without them, the world falls apart. But whenever it does, it separates into opposites, which immediately attract each other and put it together again. In the short run, fear of your opposition gives you strength and power. But in the long run, love gives you more.

So love your opposition. Then fight like hell to destroy them.

# What Do I Love?

*Wednesday, November 11, 2020*
*"Alhambra" Obsession Cracked*

Could the search for the perfect "Alhambra" be over? Have I been released? (Passive voice). Am I free of my "Alhambra" obsession? (Active voice). That would be too good to be true. Which means I wish it were.

Is that why I woke up feeling renewed? Through forced Corona retirement and time to think, have I broken my chains? I hope so. But only time will tell, since I can't trust or believe today's "feelings."

Maybe I'm just tired.

Or maybe something has really changed. A shift, even a transformation. Maybe I'll be playing guitar now for different reasons and at a different pace.

*Thursday, November 12, 2020*
*Political Writing*

I can deal with my political frustrations by writing fiction. This is "my way." I write off-beat fiction, allegories, metaphors, all indirect and biting. They are a subtle but forceful way of dealing with frustration and distilling it through fiction. I could be a "political writer" like Jonathan Swift.

Seems my choice is either to retreat to my violin room (teenage method) or deal with it "directly" by writing these off-beat stories. This idea is so preposterous, it could be right.

It certainly would help me deal with the sorrows and victories of the political world. It might even give me a reason to promote and publish my stuff! Make my political contribution by making my voice heard.

*Friday, November 13, 2020*
*Slow and Ostracized*

Could one source of my motivation to constantly improve be based on the fear of being ostracized from mankind?

Probably. One of the rewards for self-improvement is the approval, admiration, and applause of others who view that improvement as worthy and worthwhile.

Thus, you rise in esteem in their eyes, and with rising esteem comes rising acceptance and love. Welcome back to the womb. However, if you are slow and stupid, you are ostracized, kicked out, alone, on your own. Not a happy thing. In fact, terrifying and life-threatening. I suppose such a threat never really goes away but rather rises and falls with the tides of daily life. It is just one of the many quotidian pleasures and terrors.

If I play guitar slowly, I will be ostracized. Fantasy or reality, true or not, that is my long-term fear. No matter how fast I play, the fear never goes away: Speed has nothing to do with it. So practicing and playing as fast as I can never works, because the faster I go, the faster I keep running into myself. No one else really cares about my guitar speed but me. But knowing that doesn't make it any better. Awareness doesn't make it go away, but it does add some humor to the situation.

## All Is One

Why do I keep imagining the illusion of separation? Is there a hidden benefit? I don't see any. Is it a secret motivational tool? I doubt it. Or just a long-term habit, a thinking I've grown up with, a way of turning the world in my hand? I don't know.

In fact, I can see no benefit from this kind of divisive thinking. So why do it? It's all entertainment and play forms, some dangerous, others childish and playful. But whatever form the entertainment takes, we are still always and forever connected.

Why waste time and energy on the illusion of division when the reality is everyone is connected. All Is One.

## Giving up on Giving Up

I sat on my living room couch feeling very down.  I had given up.  Why?  Fog of age?  Birthday?  Done it all?  Out of gas?  I still don't really know.  When and why really don't matter.

But giving up does.

After publishing two books and finishing other projects, I may just be tired and need a rest.  "I've done it all" is my rationalization for giving myself a long break.  Today I still recognize the gnawing remnants of this malady.  But before I recognized the dangers, I was about to jump into the "give up" maelstrom.  Luckily, I caught myself, stepped back from the edge, took a deep breath, and went for a walk.  By the time I came home I had given up on giving up.

## Sunday, November 15, 2020
## Choose Hope

Every morning when I get up, and then continually throughout the day, I make the free choice between hope and hopelessness.  Hope is better than hopelessness.  At least, I think so.  Then why would I consciously or unconsciously choose hopelessness?  I might base it on my so-called "feelings," but truth is, why should I even "feel" that way?  Why should I interpret a miserable feeling or a feeling of misery as hopeless?  Seems I could just as easily interpret is as hopeful.  The attitude, even the feeling of hope or hopelessness, is a choice, my choice.

Why not choose hope?  Always.  As I wander through this illusory world, hope is so much better.

Example: Yesterday after folk dancing, my left knee hurt.  I could say, This shows I'm going downhill, my folk dance career will soon be over, old age and decrepitude are on the horizon, why bother doing anything?  It's all hopeless from here on out.  Or I could say, This pain is a directional signal, a warning, which my body is giving me.  How lucky.  It shows me I need to start or increase my exercises, strengthen my muscles, reenter the upward path to health and greater leg strength.  Also, I didn't warm up enough before the class, and my focus on my body was not strong enough during class. Tomorrow I'll begin by focusing strength-training exercises. I know what to do. I just need to do it. The choice is between down and up, cold and warmth, and light. Choose up. There's so much more blue sky and sun.

### Wednesday, November 18, 2020
### Warming Up

Maybe I can do it without warm-up and survive. But it is not my way, not best, not optimal. Best for me is about 15 minutes of warm-up for folk dancing, guitar, voice. It puts my muscles "in the mood" and prepares my mind with higher focus, creating more blood supply: Blood flow causes all to flow more smoothly.

And flowing smoothly is what I want.

### Comedian

See myself as a comedian, a stand-up comic with a stand-up folk dance teaching show, a guitar show, a one-man Dmitri Zlatov show, a walking comedy routine. Leave out my name, or change it to Dmitri Zlatov, or whatever. A radical post-Corona attitude change. Relaxing and free. Imagine the Human Comedy Bulgaria Tour, Laughing Koprivshtitsa Waltz, or whatever.

Scary? Fear reflected in sudden knee pain. Something to do with my comedy breakthrough. A comic approach would help my knees, and everything else. Leap into freedom. Truth is, by playing my Bulgarian gaida, singing folk songs, sprinkling my ad libs and more, I already have a comedy show. I just have to see it that way. An attitude change. Off-the-wall comedy. Subtle, intellectual flights of imagination that tickle my mind. Others may listen and follow but self-tickling has to be the center. And it is.

Start with fifteen minutes of funny warm up for every event. Fifteen minutes of humorous classic guitar, funny scale and arpeggio warm-up. What is humorous classic guitar? Maybe just attitude. Warming up while thinking funny, consciously missing notes and playing in a comic manner.

*Thursday, November 19, 2020*
*Comic*

I wonder if I have any talent as a comic. Wouldn't that be a fulfilling last-stage development. A wonderful way of seeing and freeing myself. Classic guitar practice is my great private love. But as a public performance, not my true talent. Maybe comedy is—my off-the-wall, zany style. Why do I resist using the word "comedy"?

I like the word *humor* better. Humor is more subtle; comedy is brash, open, in your face. Humor sneaks into your house through the back door, while comedy bangs at the front door and barges in. But maybe a bit of barging would be good for me.

*First Benefit as a Comic*

If I saw myself as a humorist, the first freedom would be: *It wouldn't matter how I played the classical guitar!* Mistakes, poor tone, flubbed notes, none of it would mean anything. No need to humiliate myself in public. And if I ever did, they would no longer even be humiliations. I'd be able to make "jokes," that is, zany comments and mental wanderings to my heart's content.

I could do it all in public! In fact, as a humorist, the barriers between private and public would fall. After all, my private mind is rather innocuous; it wouldn't insult or hurt people. The worst others might say is, "I have no idea what you're talking about!" They might lose their focus and wander off. In other words, ostracism through misunderstanding is the worst it could get.

What about big questions of fragility, aches and pains, fears, and death? Humorists deal with terrors, aches and worries. . . . Woes of life are their bread and butter. But rather than sad, under the humorist's wing, they become fun.

*Friday, November 20, 2020*
*Fear Is My Friend*

With a vaccine close on the horizon and Coronavirus coming to a close, I see stability returning to the markets, and, for the first time, a stable future up ahead, not only with fewer financial fears, but even with a sense of trading skill settling in my heart and mind. I've been through this kind of stability illusion before. But now, the fact that I am aware of it and somewhat cautious of falling into the hubris trap again gives me a bit more confidence.

In this new situation, my new fear is the fear of having no fear. What will motivate me? I know that, whether I have money or not, my mind must be occupied. If not, it will eat me up. That's the human condition. So for my own survival, with or without money, I must have something to do. Money is beside the point. All this I know.

But it has come up again. Big deal. I also know the sun will rise every day, and still every day is a new day with new directions, problems, etc. Okay, settled and onward. With my new fear of no fear, what will I do, and why will I do it?

The why is easy: If I don't use my mind, occupy it with something, idleness will destroy me. How do I fill the vacuum created by idleness? By following my miracle schedule program.

"Just shut up and do it!" is the only legitimate answer.

Evidently, I need enemies. Lethargy and inertia are good ones. Fear even better. Good enemies are the best.

*Thursday, November 26, 2020*
*The Power of Love*

What do I love about classical guitar? The touch and feel of the strings. The wholesome, rich, beautiful sound soothing my ears and relaxing my body. Legato: The feel of the strings under each finger. I slow down as I play—to find the feeling, know the feeling, and focus on it.

What do I love about languages? Feel, touch, sensation. The feel of syllables clicking in my mouth. The wild bounce and tingle of the exotic ringing through my jaw and ear bones. The taste. The tingle of each word resonating in my mouth and brain. The sight, the visual thrill, of each mysterious Hebrew, Arabic, Slavic, or Latin letter. Imagining the wild ride of meaning and thrill of competence when I master a word, phrase, complete sentence. The fun of talking to someone in this foreign language.

What do I love about singing?  The sensual sound of my voice massaging in my throat, vibrating my neck and body.

What do I love about writing?  Liberty flowing. The wild ride of my imagination running free, anywhere, everywhere, no restraints.  Loving my imagination and where it takes me.

What do I love about folk dancing?  It's similar to classical guitar: music, sounds, pleasant giggle of the body, social life (people aspect!). Now, that is different!  I can play with others.  Fun together.

What do I love about running?  Yoga (and gym)?

What do I love about tours?  Social life, people aspect?  Adventure. (I can, again, play with others.  Have fun together.  Could this be part of it?  Wouldn't that be great, if true.  Social director me.  Why do I have it?

What do I love about stock trading?

What do I love, if anything, about politics?  (Or perhaps better, what use to me are politics?  Could I call them a distracting hobby?)  Politics engross and hold me.  They "relax" me by diverting my attention.  Entertainment value?  Politics feed my anger and resentment.  (Can that be called "love?")

What do I love about leading?

It started when I lead the boys against the girls at Barnard School for Girls.  It was fun first doing things my own way, and second, doing them with others by "consulting" with them.  Mine is a subtle form: I look into everyone's eyes to see if they agree.  This is my form of consultation. I love when it works.  And it usually does.

*Monday, November 30, 2020*
*Outdoor Parking Lot Folk Dancing*

Should I write a folk dance column about how to teach outdoor folk dancing in a parking lot?  What about the fee—or rather, donation? Should it be $5.00 or $10.00?  How to decide?  One way is by asking what is best for customers.  Free folk dancing is not good for customer psychology.  Some might feel guilty about getting classes from a professional for nothing. (If they don't, they should.) A small fee assuages guilt and confers a greater sense of worth on the dancing.

It's also nice to get paid for my work. The next step above $10.00 would be $15.00, or even $20.00. Both are high. $5.00 is low but acceptable. $10.00 is good and reasonable.

What about greed? Or the happiness I get from earning lots of money? Again, I don't need it, but it would be nice. Would a price raise be good for my customers? Would it make them happy, make them feel they are not taking advantage of me, that it's fair I earn a living? We had forty people yesterday. I made good money even with the $5.00 price. It was record attendance.

What about the idea that at $5.00 per person I'm doing mitzvah work, just about working for free, following the Covid post-shut-down idea that I love teaching folk dancing so much I'll even do it for nothing! After all, this is what gave birth to parking lot folk dancing in the first place.

Will I lose that sense of love if I ask for a $10.00 donation instead of $5.00? If I raise the donation price, will I be focusing on money and forgetting about love? I don't want to forget about love, about how important folk dance leading and teaching are to me.


*Thursday, December 3, 2020*
*Secret Bandit Life: Surprise, Wonder, and Humor*

I wonder if I take a secret pride, even love, in not selling my books, in not admitting, not telling others I choreographed these dances, not telling folks I created things. Maybe I like the idea of being a stealth creator, did it behind their backs, sneaked it in, fooled them, made them laugh, while behind the scenes I was creating everything and secretly running the show. Is there a mysterious and satisfying power to living in the world this way? Mischievous, smiling brat, fooling the big brass? Maybe I like not disclosing who I am or what I do, living my public life in disguise.

This may explain why I feel uncomfortable selling and promoting my books and choreographies. It goes against my mischievous nature, and my love of the subtle, rebellious, revolutionary, illegal, bandit life.

Look at how I relish our "illegal bandit" parking lot folk dance group. I love breaking the rules, but doing it subtly, quietly, and diplomatically.

*Saturday, December 12, 2020*
*Be There: The Secret of Motivation*

I've been everywhere I need to be. There's no place left to go. Okay, so what now?

Practice guitar to seize the moment. Be in the present. Rather than "improvement," the "someday I'll be better, get it right" approach, grab the here-and-now. The moment is the grand reality.

Obviously, motivation is necessary. However, when I think of "self-improvement," I see others watching, judging, and hopefully approving of what I do.

But when I think of "seizing the moment," judgment, approval, and admiration of others disappears.

Be there and improvement will take care of itself. For highest focus, seizing the moment is the best way to go.

# New Identity

# Things Change

*Sunday, December 13, 2020*
*Starting Over*

I returned from the gym with reborn hopes of doing well. I had even done a few squats there. My knees felt like singing. I went home full of confidence and hope for a dynamic, energetic knee future. Then I sat down in the reclining chair. When I got up, I felt a sudden pain. I knew right away, it felt "different." Trouble. But why? I still don't know. I tried "working it out," but nothing happened. Swelling and pain popped out of nowhere. By the next morning I could hardly walk.

I went to my reflexologist, Lynn. She is my first line of attack. No luck. Next day I visited Dr. Archer. Strangely and happily, he said my knee was fine. Just a lot of swelling, but it would soon subside and disappear in two or three weeks. Or, if I liked, he could drain my knee, give me a shot of cortisone, and the swelling and pain would be gone in an hour. What a simple choice. "I'll take the miracle of modern medicine," I said. Sure enough, an hour or so later the pain in my knee was gone! I am now in the process of rebuilding,

The collapse of my knee may be a symbol for collapse of my old Corona shut-in and shut-up life. It's now time to rebuild, not only my knee, but everything else as well. Time for a new start.

*Thursday, December 17, 2020*
*Beauty*

Does beauty have a moral value? Sloppy is a relaxation technique that leads to beauty. Sloppy means mistakes, mistakes mean criticism, and criticism means hurtful arrows. Go past the arrows, the fear of their pain. See sloppy as a brilliant technique, a potent path to beauty.

*Sunday, December 20, 2020*
*Classical Guitar, Prayer, Public and Private Worship*

I am not religious in any outwardly organized way. Nevertheless, I am a believer. I pray alone and with others. Witness folk dancing, a public ritual of unity in a circle. But classical guitar is mostly for private worship. I play inside the walls of my inner monastery. Maybe playing classical guitar in public can only be done with the monastery and private worship in mind. Focus on the audience would then be the sin which destroys the self-expression in my performance, which indeed it does. Focus instead on the Higher Forces. Then if others, "happen to listen in," that's okay. It does not obstruct my Mount Athos personal worship form. The audience comes and goes. Higher Forces are forever. My only job is to remember them. So maybe I can pray in public as I play in public. And vice versa. My present public prayer forms are folk dance leadership, tour leadership, and teaching. My old form was giving World of Guitar concerts.

In reality, there is no separation between public and private. My "work" is my prayer form.

*Wednesday, December 23, 2020*
*Belief in the After Life is a Positive Choice*

Is there a next life? After the body dies and is cast away? Or is there something beyond? Science cannot prove it one way or the other. Religion usually has a yes answer, but it is based on faith. So what's the truth?

I'd say it comes down to personal choice. How to choose? Best way is ask: Does belief in a next life make this one better or not?

If there is no after life, "Why bother?" is king. If nothing lasts, why bother doing anything? Why improve? Why change the world for the better? This nihilistic approach does not fill my heart with joy. And I like joy. Thus, for me, best to choose belief in an afterlife. This way you work, not only in the present, but for the future as well. Improve your practice, better your situation. All good. And since everything in this world is connected, without even trying you will automatically improve the situation of others. You'll tikkum-olam your way to your own better health while creating a better life for all. It's a win-win situation.

## Saturday, January 9, 2021
## Fight On!

There is little in daily life I can control. My quotidian existence consists of focusing on those few areas I *do* control. I don't spend much time worrying about the uncontrollable. The cancellation of our president by big tech reminds me of how little power I have. Censorship and cancellation are here already. Is fascism around the corner? It all reminds me of how vulnerable I am. What, if anything, can I do about it?

One way is to focus on the few areas I have control over, make whatever changes I need, and forget about the rest. Another method is to plan an escape route. But maybe best is to stick around, stand up, and fight. This option is best for me. Fighting and inner peace go together. Fighting for what I want, what I believe in, brings peace to my soul.

Of course, I could go down in the fight. I could get hurt in the struggle, even killed. But my path has always been to stand up for my artistic and personal freedom. And this, even though my stand-up method is quiet and often camouflaged in smiling resistance backed by long-term persistence. Evidently, fighting for my values fits my personality.

I just surprised myself with this discovery. I used to think freedom meant to run away and hide in the chamber of my imagination. How do I fight the insidious censorship found in the cancellation and shutdown culture? What can, should, or, most important, will I do in my small artistic and personal world? Teaching folk dancing is one method. And I can start right away, even today. Another method is leading tours, or giving concerts, or promoting my books.

These methods are all part of my freedom repertoire. Today's cancellation, lock-down culture, with its looming shadow of fascism, only highlight their importance. Knowing I can do something, have some control, and can fight back using my way, my methods, relieves and relaxes me. It even makes me happy! You can't beat happiness.

## Tuesday, January 26, 2021

Jackson Pollock (1912–1956) was a founder of the Abstract Expressionist Movement in art. This was the first truly American art form, and had worldwide repercussions. Can a chaotic mess be called an art? Evidently, yes. Anything can be called art. It's up to you. Look at abstract expressionism. One can rationalize and glorify any mess. Why not adopt the abstract expressionist method for classical guitar? It's psychologically freeing.

## Guitar: Technique and Essence

After practicing for so many years, technique is now so embedded in my body, so much a part of my physical, mental, and spiritual self, that I can't expel it even if I wanted to. At this point in my life, technique is me. And this for better or worse.

Broken, damaged, and jagged, I am still the rock. There are many rocks like me in the world: crushed, balancing at the edge of a cliff, splintered, imperfect. It's okay. Don't worry about it. It's all part of the grand design. So relax. Enjoy your rockhood and petrification. In fact, in many circumstances, petrified is the way to go. That's just the way rocks are and were meant to be in the cosmic plan. Otherwise, why would they be there?

It's more a question of knowing what *kind* of rock I am. Metamorphic, sedimentary, igneous? The ultimate three melt-down questions are always who I am, what is my rockhood, and how to accept it.

## Mistakes and Eternity

When I hit eternity the mistakes I made will make absolutely no difference.

## Thursday, February 11, 2021
### The Lofty Purpose of Isolation

The big He wants me to go inward to discover the true secrets of guitar playing and, on the way, learn secrets about everything else. This requires a deeply inward approach. I've temporarily cancelled all businesses and outward contacts to isolate myself, rethink everything, in order to make this interior journey to the center of the Earth, and with it the center of the universe, and then expand to the vision of All is One.

Perhaps I'll go outward again. But it may not be necessary, since I'll know, deep in my bones, inward *is* outward, and vice versa.

I'm on the road to finding the source of my power. That's the meaning of my "Alhambra" search, discovered in music, through music, my original and primal celestial source.

Dare I jump in the cauldron? No choice but yes! Burn up the old self, dump it in the bin, and graciously accept the divine touch on my clothing and its grateful transfer into my new bones.

And voilá, I just played a fantastic "Alhambra"! Brilliant fiery fingers peppering and powering across the strings. Intimations of the upcoming flow of the freedom river.

### Shame and Power

What is shame but fear in disguise.
What is fear but power in disguise?
I'm on my way out of this dark hallway.
I wonder where it will lead.

### Saturday, February 13, 2021
### Guitar

I'm putting divine sloppiness above technical virtuosity, the flow of human artistic emotions above the barren desert of perfection, dropping barriers as I wade into Magic Audience River.

Roll out of the past, embrace its future, which is, of course, in the present.

# The Magic Power of Audience

*Wednesday, February 17, 2021*
*The Magic Power of Audience*

Magic happens to my focus when I'm in front of an audience. I rise to another level. Mysterious changes occur immediately. I need the magic touch of their vibrations.

Audience energy affects my body and brain. It doesn't matter whether it's for folk dancing, tours, concerts, or social gatherings. As long as they are human, it works.

I like humans.


### Life of a Folk Dance Leader

It's freezing today, and I don't want to dance.

I cancelled my outdoor dance class, using the ice-and-black-ice excuse. Some of my dancers were disappointed and expressed it in emails. I say "excuse" because I feel somewhat guilty that I cancelled. But I don't believe in guilt. And if I look further and deeper (but not too much further or deeper), I see I'm not really feeling guilty at all.

I'm feeling *angry!* First, at my dancers for wanting to dance and pushing me to run my outdoor class in this miserable cold weather.

But second, truth is, although they are complaining, they are not pushing me. I'm pushing myself, because part of me feels obligated to fulfill my commitment to run this class.

But Jim, remember, you have some rights, too! The right to not want to dance, to cancel my class because it's no fun for me in such cold weather. I'm thinking of everyone but myself. (And here I thought I was such a loner, so independent.) Actually, deep in my heart, I want to please everyone.

What about having fun?  Gone down the drain. Time to stand up for myself, to claim a privilege or two.  I don't want too many, but I need a few.

Part of leading is giving pleasure to my followers, but another part is disappointing them.

I'll just have to accept that it's part of the game.


## Wednesday, February 24, 2021
### Comedy

Humor (comedy) as a buffer or rather a weapon against hopelessness and depression.  No question my wild stories fly me away, lift me and my small mind out of these moods.  If it helps me, it will also help others out of down moods. If my flights of my imagination free me from my demons, my stories will free others, too.

If I believe this helping idea, to go beyond myself and see what I create in larger, more expansive light, I'd have a reason to promote my stories and books.  Selling them merely to enhance my ego is never enough motivation.  I never promote them. In fact, I *avoid* it.  My ego smacks me in the face, keeps me small, and prevents me from embracing my importance to others.  In fact, the thought I am important to them makes me sick.  Even the fact I *think* this way makes me sick.  Lots of sickness here.  Lots of fuel and food for humor.


## Saturday, February 27, 2021
### Fear

What have I learned from this long year of Covid?  Among other things, that fear is my stimulant.

Fears are forever and so are stimulants.  Rather than fight them, "understanding" them and trying to free myself from their grip, instead, I need to welcome them as wake-up calls.  The challenge of threat is my energy packet.  Without challenging inertia, I fall into the sleep-and-boredom state, which has its own form of unpleasantness.

As an added attraction, once I take the plunge into the pool of this challenge, focus, and deal with the problem at hand, I usually end up feeling great. So what's the problem?

## Friday, March 5, 2021
### The Grand Connector

What happens if you are separated from the world, locked in a castle, imprisoned in solitary confinement, or isolated in a cave or monastic cell? For years. How do you connect?

Does a Grand Connector exist? If not, do we need to invent one? I think so. We all need connection. And this whether one is religious, atheist, or secular. That's why my *New Leaf* is about connecting to the Magic Power of the Audience.

Seeing a physical audience does not necessarily mean you will *unite* with them. Connection is a mental and spiritual thing. It can happen even without the physical appearance of an audience. I can even connect when I'm alone anytime, anywhere, anyplace. It's part of my gene collection, my human inheritance. To connect, I only have to remember.

### Imagining My Ideal Audience

It's about imagining a new audience in my mind, one that loves and stands in awe of every classical guitar note I play. This audience is ever appreciative, amazed that I can play guitar at all. I love that audience, and they love me. And if I imagine them, they will be real.

## Monday, March 8, 2021
### Does Need Make It True?

Every morning I start off with a bout of meaninglessness. Then, mentally, I connect my purpose to others, to influencing and helping them, and my feeling of meaninglessness goes away. Every day I remind myself of this connection. Even in this Corona world of confinement, with its lock-downs, social distancing, masks, and separation, I must somehow think of ways I can influence others.

How to do that? Through vibrations of thoughts, telecommunication, and telepathy. It takes a strong belief in the power of ideas, for what are ideas but vibrations? Are thoughts really so powerful they be transmitted through walls?

Years ago, I read in a book by Vivekananda there are sages sitting in caves far removed from the world whose "job" is to think thoughts of unity and peace. The vibrations from these thoughts transmitted from their evolved brains unify the world.

I love the idea that mental vibrations are so powerful. But just because I love it, does that make it real? If I want it to be true, does that mean it is?

*Friday, March 12, 2021*
*Aim at the Audience*

It feels like a new day, and a new beginning. Aim at the audience: vocal exercises, singing, guitar playing. Also standing is more powerful than sitting. This mode, attitude, and thought process are different. I'm in their face. Dynamic, powerful, amazing. See the audience before me. (A particular person better.) Sing into their eyes. Then play classical guitar into their eyes. Toss the tones in their face. Hurl, throw the notes straight into the audience. It's aggressive, but a good first step.

Since I'm at all-or-nothing kind of guy, everything I do will now be aimed outward, at and into the audience, at and into the public, beyond my former, old and small self. It is a totally different feel and orientation. I'll be aiming outside while simultaneously going deep inside to pull out my inner-outer self.

*Include the Audience. . .Always*

Start with arm rotations. Aim them at the audience. Folk dance class is my audience, at least for now. Tours in the future, and perhaps other venues. Folk aerobics.

Telepathy: See, visualize, them in front of me. Send the vibrations of my arm rotation into their bodies. I'm using my body parts to send messages into theirs.

I do this while I'm standing in front of the class. But I can and will also do it performing the exercises alone. Think of my audience, and, from a long distance, telepathically, send them the same messages. Send them my vibrations long distance. Have the feeling and transmit it to my dancers in the parking lot far away.

This "I Am The Audience" practice definitely connects me to the world on a long-term, permanent basis. We Are Me, I Am They, They Are We.

## Monday, March 15, 2021
### Power

Rather than shame or guilt, I am *afraid* of my own power. Okay, I don't want to be anymore. Dive in. Meet and get to know my power. It's a mighty and wonderful thing, in its many manifestations.

### Creating My Own Cures

Since I create my own pains, I can create my own cures.

## Wednesday, March 17, 2021
### Distractions: Dealing with Monkey Mind

Monkey mind needs a pole, to slide up and down. Otherwise, it will destroy you. I couldn't understand the Hebrew video. The actors spoke too fast. I felt discouraged. What did I learn? Discouragement is part of the game, one of the tools of monkey mind.

Similar to cosmic depression, it is a distraction. From what? The grand healers: focus, dive in, just do it.

Drop discouragement. Dump it in the garbage bin along with cosmic depression and being overwhelmed. Instead, when these come along, look straight into them, recognize them as the sidetracks they are, and push them aside. Then dive into the task at hand. If there is none, make one up! Then just do it. The clouds of discouragement vanish. Enthusiasm steps in to take its place.

What about fatigue? It depends. Certain forms, yes; each has to be considered on its own merit. I hooked three: discouragement, cosmic depression, and being overwhelmed. Why do they arise from the playful depths of monkey mind? What is their purpose? Perhaps I'll never know.

And maybe it doesn't even matter. But they are there. The antidote to monkey mind is dive-in-and-do-it. Self-awareness is the only weapon. Enthusiasm, love, and joy are the rewards. A daily struggle, but well worth it.

# New
# Approaches

# Resets

*Friday, May 7, 2021*
*Art and Me*

Do I really care about my audience?  Or do they just annoy me, pull me away from focus on my art, by "forcing" me to focus on them?

Of *course* they are not forcing me.

A noxious element in my *mind* is forcing me to focus on them, distracting me from my main purpose: to create the light, which, once created, will fall on all around me.  The challenge is how to remember this every day.

*Sunday, May 9, 2021*
*Stepping Beyond*

Yes, I want to retire my damaged self-image, dump it in the ocean, and transition into appreciation, grab the glory of yesterday's moment when my fingers flew through, over, across, and above the ancient "Alhambra" and "Leyenda" clouds.

That moment can be remembered but never repeated.  My job is to absorb it, forget it, and move on.  Or rather *soar on!*

*Sunday, May 16, 2021*
*Advertising and Promotion*

Advertising and promotion are part of sales  So, although my videos and books bring in no direct money, they are part of the sales effort.  So is my Dance of the Week. As well as personal appearances:  Even just standing in public can be part of my advertising and promotion campaign.

## Tours and More

All my sales focus on tours. They play the central role in my sales life.

What does my folk tour business mean to me? How important is it to my psyche, to my life? More than I realized. The excitement and dynamism! Could I "sell" Hungarian words to my customers? Or for that matter, unedited journal entries? Or my computer learning process? Probably not. So what am I selling? Excitement and adventure, with a touch of exotic risk.

## The Gospel of Enthusiasm

I often avoid dealing with sour folks in the outside world because I'm afraid they may squash my enthusiasm.

But those days are over.

They may try to squash it, but I now have the confidence and strength of will to know they will fail! Nothing will squash my enthusiasm ever again! I will not let it. My sales enthusiasm used to require the consent of others. (How could I be enthusiastic, or remain enthusiastic, if they weren't?)

But this qualification is now over. My enthusiasm remains, independent of the reactions of my clients. Of course, I love when they respond with similar enthusiasm. But if they don't, my enthusiasm remains.

Enthusiasm means *en theos*, in God. That's where I want to be!

## Yes!

The "Leyenda" three-fingered arpeggio is moving beyond maintenance. This means I can improve! I can even become sensational! A sensational guitarist!

And this physical improvement can occur "even at my age." If the mind can conceive it, the body can eventually do it. But first the mind must believe it. Yes!

## Sunday, May 23, 2021
### "Some Day" Ends

I'm fooling myself. "Someday" never comes, though it does speak to a very deep need: Someday I'll be able to connect with others, my audience; someday I'll be able to perform. So, "someday," never go away. And I keep practicing no matter what. Maybe the "someday" is meant for my next life. After all, we need something to look forward to. And though we need alone time, periods of retreat, space for reflection, the desire to connect never goes away. Even for a hermit.

## Wednesday, June 2, 2021
### Accepting Success

I fear success more than failure. Sure I feel bad when I fail. But failure frees me to go wherever I want, to wander easily, aimlessly, through the fertile fields of potential. Success, on the other hand, comes with responsibility. People expect things from you, a repetition of brilliance, more success. This means mucho work, focus, concentration—stuff I like.

So what's the problem? I no longer know. Maybe there is no problem. Maybe I'm moving into a new place. Getting ready to accept success, and all the work that comes with it.

What does success mean to me? Not only that can I play guitar, but that I'm good at it. Very good. Even excellent! And that I have something to say. Why has this eluded me so long? The heavy freedom of failure is the secret brake I've put on myself for years, perhaps for most of my life. But age and maturity are whittling it away.

## Thursday, June 3, 2021
### Dealing with Success

A good day: Bookings and registrations are drifting in, business is picking up. More successes on the horizon, I'm beginning to feel overwhelmed. Success is stressful, overwhelming, with responsibility to fill orders and demands. And yet, if I can somehow get past the over-whelmed-with-responsibility feeling, I could radiate in the luxury of suc-cess. Maybe it's a question of organization. I know I'm organized, and a good organizer. That's a plus. Whenever a booking, new registration, or email comes in, it knocks my brain on its side, disorganizing my mind. Mentally regroup. Put my mental furniture back in order. Stop the mo-mentary chaos. Very uncomfortable. I hate chaos. Use my powers of organization to fight the chaos. I've succeeded in the past. Today will be no different. I'm good at organizing.

*Friday, June 4, 2021*
*Back In Business*

Last night I went to bed with a happy flutter in my heart. Why? Four new registrations for the Greek tour in October. Suddenly, instead of seeing a small tour or no tour at all, I envision the possibility of a big one, even 40 people! My business head is a whirling, foggy mess after a year and a half of pandemic lethargy. I'm starting the wake-up-and-be-alert, function-in-business process.

*Sunday, June 6, 2021*
*Improve Life by Thinking About Death*

Improve life by thinking about death. Business is picking up. Unlike the peace and free time of the pandemic, I now have lots of emails to an-swer. This annoys me because I have to answer them. It takes valuable time away from my so-called "important" activities, such as self-im-provement on guitar, so I can ultimately give a concert and stand before others as a good and improved person. Of course, in the search, I am never good or improved enough. So I have to always keep getting better in hope that someday, even posthumously, people will recognize my worth.

But suppose I end this loser view of the world. Suppose I think of answering emails as a way of embedding myself in the hearts of others, improving the world with a bit of good will? Thinking about death chains me to the importance of life and living in the here-and-now. In so doing, I'd not only improve my life, but help others in the process. An added bonus would be to enjoy answering my emails! Now that would be an amazing feat.

Death could even give me a good reason to make more videos, publish and promote my books, run tours, even give a concert. An ultimate reason to promote, not to make myself famous (the idea of death makes that concept useless and meaningless) but rather to serve others.

How does this help them? By standing as an example of how to face death with dignity, courage, purpose, and generosity.

## Tuesday, June 8, 2021
### The Truth of Motivation

For years, self-improvement, growth, learning, and curiosity have been my prime motivators. Other people rarely, came into the picture.

But now, suddenly, they have. Perhaps it's a combination of success and reading about death. Dying has always raised the question for me of "Why bother?" and "What's the use of trying, if everything ends in dust?" Irving Yalom's *Staring at the Suns,* subtitled "Overcoming the Terror of Death," suggests that leaving a legacy behind softens the blow. Note: It doesn't eliminate, only softens, it.

In my annoyance, sadness, and disappointment with the fact that I'll die, I started to search for posthumous meaning. I ended up consoling myself with the idea that I'll leave a small trail, a legacy, behind me.

But truth is, although I'll leave a legacy, naturally and simply through the organic process of living, as for motivation in the here-and-now, considering others still seems to come second. My old value system of finding what I like first comes first. When I find it, I do it, and in the doing, I start to shine. And when I shine my light naturally falls on others who may benefit. My light is my contribution. In its shining, others will benefit. Self-improvement not only creates light, but spreads it around. It's the law of the world.

I could say: *Self-improvement?* Are you *kidding?* Why bother at *this* age? But I know that's another excuse to stay home and vegetate.

And vegetation is part of the growth process, which, like all things, is transient. So *enjoy* vegetating, I say, while it lasts. And when growth shoots begin again, jump on board.

### On Leading a Folk Dance Tour

Like Moses, I am being called to lead. And it scares the hell out of me. I twist and turn, make any excuse, try to get out of it, run away. And just as Moses resisted, I resist. That's what I'm doing now. My body aches, my stomach strains, I'm stiff and weary, but I'll do almost anything to avoid facing the leadership of another tour. Making lots of money will not soothe me, although it used to help push me over the top. Learning Greek is simply another diversion, pleasant and interesting. Bottom line, I want to escape my destiny. But suffer as I do, in the end, I never run away. I am either too embarrassed or too strong. I refuse to humiliate myself. If I ever gave in and cancelled, it would destroy me. Deep down, I sense it is question of life or death. Fight and struggle. I may lose, be crushed to a pulp, even go down fighting. But I'll never die.

Lead this upcoming tour will be my glory.

### Wednesday, June 9, 2021
### Leadership

I resist leadership because it is always preceded by fear. Before diving in, I tremble in struggle. "No, no, no!" my inner gremlin screams. "Please don't make me lead. Don't force me. I'll do anything."

Anything except *not* leading.

The conflict is between my monkish, retreating, quiet, meditative inner self and my organized, smiling, enthusiastic public-service self.

Am I destined to struggle this way for the rest of my life? Probably.

### Transition

My body is stiff and aching.

I resist doing anything. I'm even feeling "satisfied" in this resistance process. What's happening? Transition. Am I creating a new body to fit my new mindset?

### Thursday, June 10, 2021
### College of Performance Anxiety

Stock trading serves as my secret escape. I use it as an excuse to avoid performance anxiety. I feel that, if I make enough money, I won't need to ever perform again, and can thus avoid this most uncomfortable, even terrible fright.

But now that the secret is out, front and center, I can see that it doesn't work.

Here's what happened to outdoor folk dancing yesterday: After the weather predicted scattered storms, I "happily" cancelled our outdoor class. As often happens, the weatherman was wrong. It remained sunny and clear all day! I felt somewhat humiliated by my decision. But outdoor folk dancing is a "flexible" art form. Changes and cancellations are subject to weather is their very nature. What can you do?

Well, actually, there is something I can do. Say no to the weatherman and simply show up for every folk dance class. Then, if the weatherman, or woe-man, turns out to be rightand it actually rains, I can always cancel my class on the spot. And if not, if the skies remain clear, we'll dance. It just means going to the trouble of showing up, which is well within my power to do. I can easily fight weather predictions.

Anyway, back to my subject. As I said, I "happily" cancelled the class. Within that "happiness" lies the problem.

Truth is, I "happily" gave in to my fear, collapsed before performance anxiety. By bowing down, giving in, not only did I not improve the situation, but I was hit by a never-before-experienced pain: A terrible sciatica-like pressure emanating from my coccyx that I felt in my lower back and butt. It came out of nowhere. I could hardly stand or walk.

This morning, although improved, the pain still hasn't gone away.

Knowing my mind, I began to suspect this was a Sarnoian TMS pain. Which means displaced anger. What was I angry at? Easy to see: The general post-pandemic fact that I have to go back to work. Business is starting up again, with all the worries, work, awe, and wonder that go into it.

## Thursday, June 17, 2021
### Performance Anxiety Continued

My guitar playing has improved to the point I can and should make YouTube videos, even perform! Big stuff. All my dreams are coming true. But some dreams are nightmares in disguise. As I work to fulfill them, part of me tries to escape in the opposite direction. What do I get for my attempts to escape? A sciatic pain in the ass.

Never give in to performance anxiety! If I do, fear turns to anger, displaces itself, and, with powerful and debilitating pain, gives me a hits me true pain in the ass. There is no escape. Only a choice.

### The Working-Retirement Solution

Can I go back to work with a total retirement and drop-out attitude? What a challenge! It certainly is the perfect post-pandemic solution. The only thing I have control of is my mind. (Even that is questionable.) An attitude change is possible but difficult!

But it must happen. If not, I'll be sentenced to eternal sciatic pain. I have to give up performance anxiety.

## Saturday, June 12, 2021
### Sciatica Walks Away

I hate to say it, or even talk about it, but the big issue I'm dealing with is death. Mine in particular, but then my wife's, and from there, my family, friends, and from there, everyone and everything else. This heavy dealing won't go away. Perfectionists like me have lots of love, but also lots of anger and anxiety. What could be more enraging and create more anxiety than the imperfection of death, which ends all self-improvements projects?

This, I believe, is at the bottom of Wednesday's sudden sciatica pain. "Why did it happen now?" I ask. I'm dealing with a heavy issue. That's why.

I'm reading *Staring at the Sun*, by Irving Yalom (means "Diamond" in Hebrew), all about death, dying, and how he and his patients deal with it. I feel a warm current of sudden relaxation flow through my body as I write this. My lower back opens up—legs, butt, and even shoulders release themselves into a deep pool of inner peace. Amazing. I know I'm on target.

# Work and Play

*Playing "Lagrima" by Francisco Tarrega*

The first challenge in my new artistic life is: How to make the guitar cry? "Lagrima" is the best place to start. It means "tears" in Spanish.

*Wednesday, June 16, 2021*

My "Gavotte en Rondeau" is still infested with speed: the disease of "I must play it fast and dazzle my opponents." This sees guitar playing as a competition rather than a personal art. The goal of guitar playing, though, is to cleanse myself of divisive competition, to empty and purify my soul and fill it with the unity of love. This is the message to bring to my next public concert. Best for me, best for others.

*Monday, June 21, 2021*

I must go back to work! No ifs, ands, or buts. Yes, I'll ache, strain, push, worry, be overwhelmed, embarrassed, humiliated, harassed by fears, blown about by countless details, fall short of my wants and re-sponsibilities, and more. But much of this happens even if I don't work. And mainly, I've solved the motivational problem. Why work? My prime reason used to be to make money.

Well, when the world returned in the middle of June and folks started to call about tours and folk dancing, I was hit with the *real* question: Why bother? Why return? Why do anything? Why not just sit around? And in this indecisive state, countless TMS pains started to plague my body. On and on: one after another. When one body part stopped ach-ing, the pains moved on to another. And I knew the indecision was kill-ing me. But I suppose I had to go through that self-torture until I realized

I had to work.

Why work? Because it's *good for me.* I flower in a work garden. Its worries, glories, anxieties, and challenges make me shine. Fighting the dragons there is much better than giving in to them. My monsters energize me, fight the opposition and rise to greater heights. This way, not only do I become my own hero, but in the struggle, my aches and pains dissolve!

*Tuesday, June 22, 2021*
*My Nature*

I can't not do a great job. It is simply not in my nature. I can only operate by giving any job my all. My hunger for self-improvement, even to reach "perfection," never stops. Awareness is my only defense.

# Land
# of Success

# Cure and Transition

### Wednesday, June 30, 2021
### Bringing the Divine Presence into the World

I used to believe that practicing positive thinking was stupid, probably because it didn't work. Whenever I tried, negative thoughts crept, slipped, then rushed in to overwhelm the effort. But now, I'm ready to try it again. A huge challenge: Taking control of my life through imagination. Try it for forty days. See what happens. I'll imagine goals of success.

### Thursday, July 1, 2021
### Dropping Question Marks

I'm dropping question marks. Why is this a huge move?

By dropping question marks, giving them up, I'm moving from doubt to definite. (And if I'm wrong, I can always reverse my decision.) What about parentheses? Not yet. . .but maybe.

### Sunday, July 4, 2021
### Terror Sparks Hope

After a month of terrible tension buffeted by the storms of indecision—should I retire, or should I return to work—my arteries decided to attack, stop the indecision pain, and let the heart make the decision for me. I started writing like crazy in order to understand myself. What would motivate me? Will I ever return to folk dance teaching, running, yoga, gym, and exercise? If I did, will it only be for my health? What about fun and joy?

Except for trading stocks, which is really a sedentary sport, money no longer interests me. Health might work. After all, its etymological root is "whole."

I need a calling. Could health be a new calling? What about thoughts of superiority and arrogance? I feel somewhat naked without them and revealed as the sensitive, vulnerable person that I am.

Out the window is also "strong and dynamic." I hate to lose it. Can I ever get it back? Or is that question another form of put-down? After all, I am facing a real challenge. Also, remember, I wanted a fresh start, a new life. And voilá, I have one! (And I didn't even have to make a choice.) I now have a good excuse or "reason" to stop, give up my tours and folk dance classes.

Certainly, if I return, I'll need new and fresh reasons to do so. At the moment, I have none. But it is still too early to tell.

I trembled in panic. But could this fear, felt deep in my gut, be the first shot of energy, one that will fuel my future?

Veiled by terror, lying deep in the solar plexus, this shot of fear could be optimism in disguise, an explosion of hope in a new landscape. If I trust my instincts, this seed of terror seems like the beginning of my new life.

### Dance of the Week

Since Corona has shut down my folk dance classes, and destroyed my international folk dance tours, and I am truly out of business, should I still bother sending out Dances of the Week? Or leave the field, at least for a while? Or see this Corona shut down disaster period as a hiatus, a transitional time of reflection to figure out my next direction? Meanwhile, I'll keep my options open by continuing to send out the dances. It's easy to do.

But is it honest? If I do, am I tempting others to join folk dance classes or register for tours that no longer, and may never, exist?

### Monday, July 5, 2021

Do clotted arteries equal a clotted mind? More important, does the mind create clotted arteries? Mine has been cluttered by indecision about how and what to retire in my life. And this really began after the two-month anger-and-panic period at the beginning of Corona. Since then I have been asking, how will I change my life?

Of course, this was just a theoretical problem during Corona. There was no work anyway and thus no real possibility of making a choice. But that all changed in June, when tours and folk dance classes opened up. I had to make a real decision.

Should I return to teach folk dancing at Goldens Bridge? Or not? I was incapable of deciding. Yes, no, maybe, back and forth every day. Living daily in the vise, squeezed by these opposites, with no definite decision in sight, drove me nuts. It created countless muscle pains in my body, and a brand-new one between my shoulder blades.

This brought me to the doctor, a stress test, three clotted arteries, stents, and the beginning of the new attitude I long ago wanted to find.

I couldn't make the decision. So the doctor made it for me. "You have to cancel your Goldens Bridge classes for at least two weeks."

I was devastated. "I can't do that," I said. "Tonight is opening night. All our dancers will be there. I can't go back on my word, my commitment and obligation. They'll all be disappointed."

"You have to cancel," she said. "There is no choice. Unless, of course, you want to take a chance of dying."

So I called Goldens Bridge and cancelled.

(It all eventually worked out. Michael and Cindy took over, ran the night, and the folks there, although some were shocked by my sudden cancellation, still had a good time dancing. And this will continue in the future.)

But getting back to me: Were my clotted arteries a long time in the making? And did I, or part of me, "create" the situation, clog my own arteries during the process and thus force others to make this extremely difficult choice for me? Did I do it to protect myself from something even worse, namely to bravely and courageously give up my beloved Goldens Bridge?

As I read Hebrew this morning, I feel a bit dizzy. Is this a real, new dizziness created by my new situation? Or does it arise from a hidden terror; the sudden loss of all my power and a new self-concept as a (temporary, I hope) invalid? I'm puzzled and humbled, frightened but peaceful.

What a strange new combination. I'm frightened by this apparent loss of power. Note the word "apparent." It means I'm not sure why, or even if, I have lost it. Maybe I'm at the edge of a new power. Who knows where this will lead?

But along with this fear, I'm also fascinated by how my mind works.

Part of it has separated itself and stands beside me, observing, looking down with great curiosity, trying to figure out how my thought process works. It chronicles the continuing adventures of a mind, in this case, my own.

It is the reason for this *New Leaf Journal* and its journal-writing process.

### New Power

Due to the total breakdown of my old life, I could be at the cusp of a new power. I wonder if this is true. Secretly, I sense it is! Is this too brash and arrogant to say? Or do I now simply have more faith in my intuition?) Let's say I'm right. If I'm giving birth to a new self, why wouldn't a new power come with it? What might this new power be? Spiritual? Mental? Physical? A combination of all three? Other?

Is this hubris, or am I just getting smarter? Scary in its magnificence.

### Clogged Arteries

Open up blocked arteries. What a symbol for opening up the Flow of Power, *my* power—stopped, stymied, and inhibited but now blown open by this dynamic post-Covid cover, sewer manhole explosion.

Start with guitar, and the birth of Mighty Wrist. But it doesn't end there.

### The Adventures of Mighty Wrist and the Dynamite Heart

Slow, focused, and strong, or fast and dynamic, Mighty Wrist flying under and over notes, flowing through blood streams, unclogging arteries, clearing veins, as he builds the Dynamite Heart Artery-clad in green dynamite the scarlet, stent-carrying, dye-ensnarled Mighty Wrist rushes to save his beloved Violet from the razor-toothed jaws of Big Dragon Charlie Pipesqueak. Tuning up his antlers and rubbing his salted crotchifier, the knighted Hero of the Unusual, supported by an army of ulnas, marches across Follicle Field, catching hairs with every footstep.

"Never mind the music," says Mighty Wrist. "It's fun fingers flying that counts!"

### Wednesday, July 7, 2021
### The Divine Presence

Questions go on forever. Answers are tough. Does life have a grand purpose? That's the big one. But few agreed on the answer precisely because it is *the* question.

So as I sit here, wondering, does life have a grand purpose?" I think so. I agree with the Jewish philosophy of *tikkun olam*. The purpose of mankind (and womankind) is to heal the world. One way (perhaps the only way) is to bring the Divine Presence down to Earth. How do I know about the Divine Presence? Through music. It is exactly what I felt as a teenager, playing violin in my room and had those great melt-down experiences listening to Beethoven symphonies and more. As I broke down in tears of joy, I absolutely knew there existed a Higher Power, a Magnificence guiding the world.

Growing up in a secular family, I never told anyone about these experiences. They would have thought I was crazy. Why subject myself to ridicule? Why sully the vision of such a beautiful connection to what I would later call the Divine? Why put my pearls before secular swine to be mocked and destroyed? I couldn't take such a chance. So I stayed mum.

But deep in my unstented heart, through the experience of music, I knew a higher power existed. This knowledge gave me the strength and courage to pursue my dreams, endure, move on despite obstacles and hardships. I'd do the things I loved because I knew that love connected me to the Grand Magnificence and, through its healing power, to all others.

The next two big questions are: What do I *want* to do, and what *can* I do? I'm not sure which comes first. Perhaps they cannot be separated. A good starting point is to consider the thought that the power of wanting makes all things possible.

Is this realistic? Don't people have limitations? Yes. As Rick says, "There are limitations. Only no one knows what they are!"

## Prophet

I'm writing like a prophet. Quite amazing. What is even more amazing is that I'm not amazed. Is being a prophet the next step? How bold, arrogant, and hubris-filled is such a question! Yet I just asked it. But perhaps calling the idea an act of hubris is just another old-neighborhood way of putting it down.

Okay, suppose being a prophet *is* the next step. Lots of humans have become prophets. Why not me? Is it really such a big deal? I'd see it as a great honor and be very proud to possess the calling, without the ego pride, but with humility.

Perhaps it's a question of "getting used to it," thinking of myself in a new way. Could unclotted arteries lead to unclotted mind and, from there, to an unclotted spirit and a clear pathway to the higher powers? Sounds possible, reasonable, and right. I tremble at the thought. But trembling is good.

## Thursday, July 8, 2021
## The Cure

Joy is the ultimate medicine. It is the cure that burns away all ills. But how do you find it? Where do you get the stents to widen the arteries so joy can freely flow through them? Start with mild pleasure. Then put some into my knees.

## Monday, July 12, 2021
## Crossing the Line

I'm trembling because I must submit to the Voice, humble my little self, lose, give up, drop my ego. Submerge. Surrender to the Voice. I'm not angry, but afraid. By giving up and giving in, I'll fall straight into the loving arms of the Abyss. That's what arteries stuffed with plaque are all about. A call and a calling. Pay attention to the Big Guy. God loves you. He will give you All. But first listen and submit. I feel a bit embarrassed. Fooled by Ha Shem. What would my secular, communist family say? What would Ma say? "You're a fool, a dope. Stupid, stupid! Only idiots and soft brainers believe in such trash. I can understand submitting to Lenin, or Stalin, but God? Forget it. How stupid can you be? Only fools worship God and religion. Come back home. Worship the Truth with us at the International and One-World Order.

I have crossed the line with deepening vision, I'm breaking all the family rules, boundaries, and traditions, stepping outside the box—*way* outside, becoming a crazy mystic religious, a Hassid of the worst order. I am turning away from the red star, conversing with the Higher Power. Total ostracism.

Okay, Ma, you're right. But what's the trade-off? I get to play "Alhambra"! After that, He'll throw in the audience. I could end up with a fearless life.

What's the message? Give my heart to Big A, and my arteries will follow. Blood will flow through my body, delivering oxygen to every prison cell. Bars will fall. Everyone will walk. Not bad for a mere conversion. It's all so good and healthy.

I like working with Big Guy. He'll also soften worries about death and fragility. In fact, He'll take care of Everything. All I have to do is submit. Not a bad deal. Moses was right.

## Tuesday, July 13, 2021
### I Miss My Arrogance

Feeling good this morning. Humbled, having lost some arrogance, I miss it. Why *was* I arrogant? Fear? Ego? Now just like everyone else, vulnerable.

Arrogance gave me a wonderful illusion of invincibility. How great was that! And didn't the beautiful dream of being unlimited give me the courage and strength to extend my boundaries, try crazy things, step out of the box, run that extra mile or hour, explore crazy destinations, go beyond that limit, through that closed door, through boundaries, and aim for the sun?

But my arrogance has slipped down the drain. Can I find another source of strength and courage on the level plains of humility?

## Saturday, July 17, 2021
### Fun Heals the World

Hard to believe that the "selfish act" of enjoying my guitar playing helps others. But it does—through the shining process. Whet the sun shines, it shines on everyone. It's a cosmic law. If I help myself, I automatically help others. And this whether I think about it, want it, or not.

It's such a paradox. I thought I was a fun guy. Lots of smiles as I social direct, dance with guests and customers, talk with friends. And it's true—I not only have a born talent to enjoy and lead others; I like the bantering process.

But deep in my soul, I won't allow my personal self to have fun. In private my goal is to constantly improve, get better because it is my job to take care of others and heal the world. And until I am perfect, and until I am perfected, I cannot do my job well. I can't take care of others and heal the world. The paradox is: If I could allow myself to have fun, to roll with my fun index finger, to frolic when emailing, to allow myself to enjoy each step of these processes, I'd heal the world and take care of others even better!

That is the beauty of artery-clearing stents. By uncluttering this oxygen-bearing passage, cleaning out the plaque, symbol of accumulated mental garbage, I am clearing a pathway to personal fun!

### Visiting Hell Strengthens My Resolve

I'm afflicted by periodic visits to the negative neighborhood of discouragement, emptiness, purposelessness, death, and "Why bother?"

A visit from the devil himself. Does he appear just for me? Should I feel flattered by such personal attention?

*Wednesday, July 21, 2021*
*Dizzy with Wonder*

"Dizzy" comes from a Dutch/Germanic root meaning "stupid." "Stupid" comes from Latin "stupido," meaning wonder. Am I dizzy with stupidity, dizzy with wonder? If I am and fall on the floor, what a wonder-full way to collapse! But I don't want to collapse. I want to enjoy.

Is enjoyment so difficult?

*Friday, July 23, 2021*
*Devil Questions*

Some questions are merely fancy ways of depressing myself. They cannot be answered. They probably should not even be asked. It is the devil's job to throw you off and bring you down. One of his methods is to pose unanswerable questions whose purpose is to depress you. Questions like: Why must we all die, or Why are all things transient?

Limitations exist. Figuring out eternal life is a toughie. So far no one knows what to do about it.

*A Concert of Good Vibrations*

Is playing guitar in person important? After all, I can send out good vibrations by playing alone in my room. Why bother playing for an actual audience? Isn't a virtual one enough? How about an invisible one? Is the desire to play for a live audience simply an ego trip? One where I need to prove myself by hearing applause, seeing smiles?

*Saturday, July 24, 2021*
*Patient*

Yesterday I started the cardio rehab program in Hackensack Hospital. My old life and self-definition have been blown away. I am now, and see myself as, a patient, a sick person who needs to be cured.

Of course, on one level, I am no different from the person who existed yesterday. But still a corner of myself believed I was above the ordinary trials and tribulations of life. And loved believing it! Now that's all gone. I am walking on the treadmill with everyone else.

## Heart Attack

What to do when the heart attacks? Go on offensive: Attack it back!

Treat it like monkey mind. When monkey mind jumps from one thought to another, pushes you around—which is almost always—push back! Put the monkey back in the tree where it belongs. Put the heart back in place. Don't let it out of its pericardium.

## Sunday, July 25, 2021
### Adventures of Index Finger

I am giving my right index finger some time in the sun for recognition and light, and love, for its slow-giving power, its constant support during years of beating and abuse as its power remained camouflaged in the background, a quiet grandfather, never giving up, always supporting my slower self.

Fast self is my dynamic, jumpy self, exuberant, radiant, wild, and funny, tittering on the edge, bordering on ecstasy, ready to jump off a cliff—ungrounded, fly or float, wild and untamed, in the stratosphere.

Slow self is my deep, wise one, with mellow joy bordering on contentment.

Can slow, wise self and fast dynamic fast self merge in the index finger? Can different attitudes, with their separate states, merge into a united states? Can the schizophrenic become monophrenic? Can the many become one? Stay tuned as daily new adventures of index finger unfold.

## Friday, August 6, 2021
### Confusing Threads Among the Goodness

Why did my teeth hurt yesterday? Terrible pain. I called my dentist for an emergency meeting.

But this morning the pain is gone!  Why?  What happened?  Are my teeth a real problem?  A distraction?  But if the latter, a distraction, distraction from what?

I had a good day yesterday.  Actually, mentally, my trading was the best!  So what, aside from my teeth, is the problem?  Could it be that there is none, that I just took my first, confused steps into the new Attitude-and-Style Land.

So maybe my teeth were a distraction, created to throw me off the Good Attitude path.  And there's the thought that my August foray into chemistry, biology, and anatomy may have run its course, served its purpose.

Let's start with the goodness and the All-Good Day. And see if I can stick to it and follow its attitudinal and stylish footsteps.

I'm picking up my guitar right now.

# Leadership

### Saturday, August 7, 2021
### Performance Anxiety Down the Drain

Here's an amazing realization: I'd rather fear my audience and feel performance anxiety than express the overwhelming love I have for them. In the process, I lose myself, ego disappears, self dissolves in a sea of Love.

Lose my ego? Give it up? Are you kidding? I'd never dare to do such a thing in public. In private, yes, but in public, never. Most of my life, I've chosen to keep my ego within its tight shell. Of course, while ensconced in this self-created prison, I still feel the love of audience. But I do not *express* it. Of, if I do, it is only very indirectly.

This greatly hinders my art. It puts fear in the place of love. Am I ready to express the vulnerable truth of love in public? I'd like to. Maybe my performance anxiety is the fear of expressing love.

And the eternal is found in love.

### The "Dare to Dance!" Political Party

Jim Gold, head of the Folk Dance Party, has decided to run for president. But before he does, he'd like to offer his new post-covid "Dare to Dance" program. In this time of political division, health fears, and cancel culture, our "Dare to Dance!" program offers a refreshing solution to separation of all kinds.

First, we are not a right or left party. Instead, we go in all directions, right, left, forward, back, sidewards, even diagonally. Also we go up and down with jumps, squats, digging movements, and a few lying-on-the-floor steps.

We accept all people. We don't care how you think, feel, or look. We love the vaccinated and unvaccinated, tall and short, fat and thin, smart and dumb, he/she/they, him/her/them. The only folks we do not accept are the financially obstinate who refuse to pay our $10.00 entrance fee.

### Guitar

If I believe in Sarno's TMS (tension myonitis syndrome), what is my performance anxiety hiding? Why did I create it? What does it distract me from? From performance audacity! It shields me from my boldness and courage, determination, persistence, and aggressive "fuck 'em all" approach, my "I'll do it anyway, no matter what anyone says," my rebellious "I'll do what I want!" spirit.

Performance audacity indeed. And my history proves me right. Otherwise, I couldn't have had a guitar concert performing career. But I gave up my performing career, or rather put it on hold, in order to "perfect myself."

Now, after forty years of searching in the desert, I'm still not perfect, but I've found my answer to performance audacity. Go for it!

### Winning the Glory Prize

I don't lose unless I aim higher and try moving past what I already know. Thus, so-called failure, losing, means I'm making an effort to move up the ladder. And climbing the ladder has its own glory.

### Find Happiness in Losing

Although it can be depressing, losing can be more motivational than winning. Winning is a resting place. Where do you go after you win? Winning is glorious, but only for a short time. The sunlight at the top of the mountain can last minutes, hours, days, even weeks. But eventually the light fades. Boredom and listlessness set in. Slowly, you start heading downhill. The long-term road of satisfaction is the road up. And this road has failure en route. Hopefully, with this realization, I'll learn to be happy when I lose.

*Monday, August 23, 2021*
*Optimism on Becoming a "Was"*

As I read about the next generation of folk dance teachers, I have a strange sensation that I'm slipping out of history, fading into the past. The feeling is beyond bad or good but rather strangely distant. Peaceful, philosophical, protective, it is highlighted by my indifference to folk dancing on Zoom.

I'm on the way to a different place. Perhaps I'm there already. Of course, the river never stops flowing. My "was" will turn into a "will be." But what will I be? Fading out does bring perspective. A new significance may rise from my insignificance. By mattering less, things and events soon may matter more. In the process, ego fades into oblivion. The old self burns slowly, then falls apart. New powers of focus, concentration, and perspective are rising from its ashes.

*Tuesday, August 24, 2021*
*False Divisions*

Harry Berlow was my first Flamenco guitar teacher. Rolando Valdes Blaine was my first classical guitar teacher. Like so many I know and studied with, they died years ago. Can one dedicate pieces to the dead? Why not? After all, like the terms "classical guitar" and "folk guitar," the words "living" and "dead" are, on the deepest level, really false divisions.

*Talking to my Knees*

Talk to my knees. Give them commands. Show them who's boss. Wag my finger and tell them: "I'm the boss, the leader. I'm too busy to bother with you. Get back into your corner! Shut up and leave me alone!"

*Friday, August 27, 2021*

One reason I don't take credit for the folk dances I choreograph is I'm afraid folks will not like the dances. So fear of criticism is my "explanation" for not taking credit.

But there may be a higher reason. Maybe they are better "without ego." When I dance and teach, unhindered by ego and all its self-protecting concerns, my life purpose of healing and bringing joy to others can enter more easily.

### Saturday, August 28, 2021
### Allow

The new word of the day is "allow." Allow the infinite to enter. Start with the Allow-hambra; the whole right arm (*yad hazak*, "the strong arm" in Hebrew) opens, relaxed, and allows the Power to enter through the right wrist. Right shoulder is the flow shoulder. Power flows through the relaxed right wrist and fingers.

So far the left shoulder is the resistance shoulder. That's why it hurts.

### Sunday, August 29, 2021
### Allowing the All in All-ow

The infinite present includes me, the audience, and everything else animate and inanimate. No divisions. It includes All. In other words, the audience is *always* present. In vibrational reality, it is around me even when I am alone. Thus, I am wasting my time practicing to improve in order to be more perfect when I finally "perform" before my audience.

### Improvise!

When I teach folk dancing, or perform in general, what happens when I forget my material in public? What should I do? Improvise! Drift. Wander off into another speech. Play some jazz and new chords. Whatever. Forgetting in public, then improvising your way out, is a great favor, encouragement, and teaching for the audience. It shows them no forms are fixed. Handling your memory lapse by improvising on the spot demonstrates the grand truth that creativity, spontaneity, and improvisation rule the present.

*Monday, August 30, 2021*
*Johann Sebastian Bach's Body*

Johann Sebastian Bach's body is dead, decomposed, and gone. But I see the real him, his spirit as part of the Infinite. I allow myself to connect with his spirit.

If I slip and forget, and I probably will, best is to re-engage, retreat, and re-engage.

*Tuesday, August 31, 2021*
*The Practice of Self-Love*

As the key to community, self-love is not selfish. Rather, it is the All-Is-One meditation practice, a universal love form, often hidden and disguised. Self-love is the key and foundation. With its wisdom and practice, everything falls into place.

*Guitar Meditation Concert*

Visualize a concert with no applause. Not one clap. The audience simply sits quietly in meditation.

There are dual aspects to applause. It separates audience and performer, reminding them of their division. But it also unites audience and performer in the joy of appreciation.

*Monday, September 6, 2021*
*Segovia Was Right*

It was all about a grand fifty-year fight between my ego and Andres Segovia. The battleground was the "Alhambra." My way was the treble.

His way was the bass. I fought for treble domination for forty-five years. And lost. Truth is, and always was, the "Alhambra" melody was in the bass. Segovia was right. I finally gave in, gave up, lost my battle.

But I won the "Alhambra"! With melody in the bass, I'm playing it well.

### Thursday, September 9, 2021
### The Greatest Rule

The greatest rule for guitar playing—and life—is there are no hard and fast rules. Play guitar with "no rules in mind." See what happens.

### Wednesday, September 15, 2021
### World of Guitar Revisited

I put some of my old VCR videos on thumb drives, so l could see them on my computer. Luckily, one of the videos was a children's performance of my World of Guitar school program given at the Pine Lakes School in Wayne on 1986. I watched my old self perform. I was great! Easy, fluid, personality style. *Most* amazing, my *guitar playing was great!* Clear, fast, competent, no mistakes or flubs, lively and dynamic.

Hard to believe how good I was. I can say it now. I'm nearly forty years away from that performance. I was looking at another person. And to my happy amazement and pleasure, the old "I" seemed to play better than the new one of today. And this after decades of practicing to improve!

What happened? Why did I bother practicing all these years? Why did I have such an inferiority complex? Why did I give up my performing career in order to "improve?" Evidently, I was great to begin with. Only I didn't realize it. Although others knew, recognized my skill and my talents, and hired me to perform, and I ended up making a good living performing, I certainly didn't see it myself.

I had a huge inferiority complex to deal with and conquer, and no doubt that's why I ended up taking all that time off to so-called self-improve. During this long process, I can't say I've improved at all. I have, through leadership in folk dance and tours, discovered self-confidence. (But note: guitar practice didn't give it to me!)

### Thursday, September 16, 2021
### Over and Over

Practicing something over and over and over and over and over and over and over and over again creates a qualitative difference. It opens new doors, reveals new realities, and changes forever the way you do or see things.

Yes!

"Leyenda" C bar and three-fingered arpeggio: the relaxation problem is in the left hand (not the right). I can play with raised thumb, too.

This means I'm moving beyond maintenance. I *can* improve; I *can* become sensational! Wow. And this improvement can happen "even at my age." This means such breakthroughs can occur in running, yoga, fifties, calliyoga, folk dancing, all.

If the mind can conceive it, the body can (eventually) do it. But the mind must first believe and envision it. Yes!

Is the ability to improve and become sensational possible in other fields as well? I'm sure it is. But each one takes energy, focus, and years of training. Obviously, I can't do them all. But I could focus on the few I love.

### Risks. . .of Injury: A Strange Form of Motivation

By trying to warm up faster on the guitar or running, yoga, and calli, I am taking on the risk of injury. But it is the risk itself, the excitement created by standing at the edge, that drives me on.

# Creating the Eternal Fun Life

*Monday, September 27, 2021*
*Brain Re-wired? Yes!*

During the past Corona year and a half my brain has been slowly re-wired. It is difficult, maybe impossible, for me to go back to the way I was.

I am different now—fresh, new, redone, whole. I can move with confidence, fun, boldness, and a string of wahoos into the new world. I just have to hang around, be myself, watch it all happen effortlessly.

*Thursday, September 30, 2021*
*Fun in Writing: New Goals and Commitment*

I've rethought my commitment to writing. What did I come up with?

Two goals emerged for this year: (a) publish another *New Leaf,* write another book of fiction. To accomplish this make a new morning-hour-a-day commitment to writing!

To find the time to do this, I will have to replace stock trading with writing. Of course, I've known for years that trading stocks has been my major *distraction* from writing. Why did I need such a distraction? Do I still?

I have reached the end of distraction. It's a new life, a new time, a new me. Time to dive into the *Fun of Writing!*

Should I give up trading stocks? That would be quite sad. I'd be losing a fun pastime. Of course, I know it's only fun when I win, and most the time I lose, money. And losing is no fun. I am in a new place, ready to create a new life plan. And writing has to be a part of it.

During the post-stent period, I've found fun in classical guitar playing. I want to add fun in writing, then find more fun in other pursuits.

## Scary, but Glorious: No Going Back

I'm on the cusp of waking up after so many years of practice in the trenches. Like a snake, I'm slipping out of my old skin. Scary, but glorious. I'm realizing every guitar dream. Out of my cocoon, fluttering, no going back from waking, no passage out of this molten state.

It's hot, strange, solid, and dreamy. Accept it, and move on. My body is broken and dripping, but that's how a butterfly feels before its first flight.

## Sunday, October 3, 2021
## A Radical Thought

If All-Is-One is true, if the earthly life and astral "life" merge, there is no such thing as life or death. These terms are human definitions, distinctions; we separate things, break them into smaller pieces to better understand them. But in reality, on the broadest, highest spiritual plane, all things are connected. So life and death are earthly, material distinctions, and on the Highest, not real. Seeing them as separate makes us suffer. To see all as connected brings peace of mind. And with the mind at peace, healing of the body, peace of body, follow.

Every moment, although unique, is connected to the Whole. By its very nature, it merges, then rolls into the Infinite. Our terrestrial job is to awaken, and know.

## Thursday, October 7, 2021
## Folk Dance Class Vaccination Solution

Trust and love go together. My folk dance flier says "Masks and vaccination required." What do I say when someone asks: "Is everyone here vaccinated?"

My answer: "Yes, everyone is vaccinated."

"How do you know?" they ask. "Did you see their vaccination cards?"

My answer: "They told me they are vaccinated. I trust them."

*Friday, October 8, 2021*
*Luxuriating in Regret (Melody Is in the Bass)*

I luxuriate in regret. I spent decades denying the bass and focusing on the treble while playing the "Alhambra." Thus, I could never play it.

But this inability "allowed me" to start the tour business.

Without my "Alhambra" problem, I never would have built my tour business. So the result is I have a guitar regret along with a tour business victory. Plus I made enough money in the tour business that I can now focus on guitar and "Alhambra."

So luxuriate in the regret of forty years spent in the "Alhambra" Tremolo desert. Maybe that was the purpose of my exile.


*Monday, October 11, 2021*
*Learning Vibrations*

Since everything is connected, when I learn a Hebrew word, or anything else, the whole world "learns" it along with me. This is the universal beauty of study. Study and learning create pleasant, expansive, fun, positive molecules. When I study, I unconsciously (consciously, too) spread these molecules deep into the maw of the vibrating universe. A worthy practice.


*What is my Purpose*

What is my purpose? Spreading joy in this hurting and damaged world. How? First heal myself. Once successful, spread the news through my art and organizational forms.

Joy includes the tears of catharsis, peals of laughter, and an occasional belch.


*The Purpose of Depression*

Depression is the loss of connection to others. De-pressed, pressed down, lost, lonely, sinking into a pit of despair, meaninglessness. Its purpose is to reconnect you. Depression ends when the knowledge that we are all connected is remembered. Then it is replaced by curiosity and thankfulness.

Mercy is reconnecting. That's why the French say, "Merci."

### Friday, October 15, 2021
### Singing is So Much Fun!

Singing is so much fun!

So are my bits, off-beat comedy, stories, and quirky humor. So much fun!

Maybe I am really not afraid of audience criticism. Maybe I've been afraid of the fun! The fearless abandon, diving in, having a great time! Maybe I've been hiding behind classical guitar inadequacies and my invented problems.

Time to come out of hiding, take off the mask.

### Saturday, October 16, 2021
### My Stock Market-Trading Self

Stock market trading is much more important and meaningful to me than I want to think. Money, security, success and failure are all very emotional. Plus I must like it, love it, if I willingly spend so much time at it.

This morning I suddenly felt chilled, feverish, and sick. This is rare. "Why now?" Immediately yesterday's stock market trading success came to mind. Yesterday was my best trading day in months! (Maybe years?) Seemed everything I touched turned to gold. I was secretly thrilled, stunned, amazed, and gloriously happy. But I suppressed these feelings. The happy thoughts reversed direction, and instead of helping me celebrate, gave me chills, fever, and made me sick.

I don't want to be sick. And there is no reason to be sick—unless I suppress my real feelings. Which are total Wahoos! So today, I must reassess my stock market trading.

How I love it! And how I love succeeding at it! I love and am fascinated by trading stocks.

What is the result of this grand acceptance and personal revelation?

Maybe stock trading is the interest, love, passion, career, and new job that will "replace" tours.

How can I think such a thing when in the past, I've been so bad at it? Always losing money, or at best, never making any. And this happened year after year. Even during these Corona years, when I totally dedicated myself to trading.

Yet I kept doing it, stuck with it, never giving up. Is this a sign of love and passion, despite failure? Maybe. For some reason, trading is fascinating and important to me. It is contrary to my background—no history of trading or even interest in my family. How did this happen? How did such an interest arise?

From playing in the park? From being mischievous, robbing mailboxes when I was a kid, having a sense of humor and adventure? All of the above. Perhaps yesterday's success was a teaching moment, a subtle message send down by HaShem Himself to clearly reveal a new pathway for the new me.

In any case, I have the bug, passion, love, and interest. And this continues through failure or success. Go with it, see what happens.

I wanted something new. Maybe it has been right in front of me all along. I want more stock market trading success. I can only get it by facing failure. Which I certainly have done.

# Tikkun Olam Equals Pride and Glory

*Saturday, October 30, 2021*
*Purpose*

Whenever I have no purpose, my body hurts: Aches and pains pull it apart. But whenever I have a purpose, it unites my disparate energies, draws them into one stream, makes me one and whole again. And when I am whole, my pains disappear!

*Tuesday, November 2, 2021*
*Love My Anxiety*

Anxiety is forever. So is Love. It is my teacher and friend. Love of anxiety easily replaces love of money. As I say, the former is forever, the latter transient and "curable."

How to love anxiety? Last night I used it before leading our folk dance class. Just before it, I had pain in my legs and right foot. I could hardly walk. And the class was starting in ten minutes!

I meditated hard on my pain, thought about *Nestinarsko horo,* the Bulgaria fire walker dance in which dancers walk barefoot across hot coals. Due to their powerful pre-walk meditations—which sometimes last a day or more—they feel no pain. And miraculously, the coals do not burn their feet!

Last night I did something similar. I thought about Nestinarsko as I meditated upon my foot; I focused my mind on the upcoming class. It worked. I felt no foot or leg pain during class. And I gave a great class! A great evening ensued! And note: The moment my class ended, all my foot and leg pain returned! Suddenly, I could hardly walk again! What does this say about the power of mind? And the power that pre-performance anxiety gives me? It forced me to rise above my imagined limitations, perform, and create a great class!

*Hero Worship: Proud of My Fear*

I've always been secretly proud of my fear.  I take pride in owning and dealing with it. It makes me my own hero.

I like heroes.


*Friday, November 5, 2021*
*Guitar: Sor Etude Number 12*

Speed is glorious.  Expression is glorious.  Can I combine them, melt them together in one grand and glorious Glorious?  I have to get used to this new land of speed.

My Angel
Is all my guitar playing
Only to win her
Express my love
For my angel.
On many planes
She is with me
Flying together
Live in the moment
Always is now
Know and remember this
So un-fearful and soothing
Nice to know


*Saturday, November 6, 2021*
*The Divine Purpose and Plan*

A couple of years after I started classical guitar lessons with Alberto Valdes Blaine, I could easily play "Alhambra," "Leyenda," my flamencan pieces, and more.  And in fact, I did perform them publicly.

No problem beyond the usual pre-performance anxiety.

Only after I decided to improve, which meant dispel my pre-performance nervousness, that I stopped being able to play these guitar pieces. Mine was a self-induced paralysis.

But now I think it was all part of the divine plan. I had to suffocate my performing talent in order to gain self-confidence by going in other directions.

And I did—by developing leadership, organizing skills, and confidence in tours, folk dancing, and weekends. All the while thinking that *someday* I'd be able to play guitar and give a great concert.

Well, those days are now here. What has changed? Now I love my anxiety, my pre-performance fear. I see it as a grand motivator energizing body, focusing my mind.

Also, my confidence has risen. I know how to lead tours, run folk dance classes, and write books. I'm ready to revisit my past, straighten it out, do it better, come back stronger.

Someday my books may be read, and I will become famous. Or maybe no. But since All-Is-One, whether it is now or posthumously, or never doesn't matter. I will always be known, recognized and famous on the astral plane. And this as inner terrestrial development rolls along.

## Sunday, November 7, 2021
### The Gift of Fear

Yesterday I ran "somewhat well." It was the first time I'd run in over four months! Wonderful! But as the day progressed, I realized I felt "afraid" about getting back into running. But now I thought differently: perhaps this fear, and even fear in general, was a good thing.

What's new? Seeing fear as a good thing. Also starting over—from scratch. Move slowly, and with caution. Why? Because I'm bringing lots of new attitudes to the table.

One biggie is seeing fear as a good thing. This as I read a great book: *The Gift of Fear*, by Gavin de Becker.

I'm ready for it. As I re-enter the world, I'm using my fear, along with love, as positive energy and motivation sources to propel me into tikkun olam.

### Guitar, Running, Folk Dancing

Things happen at speed that don't happen in slow. Practicing fast is a different mode from practicing slow. Both reveal aspects of the self. I've practiced in slow mode for many years. Time to add fast. Fast is a new world. Get used to it.

### Guitar: "Alhambra," Tremolo

Relaxed and beautiful thumb. Take control of this deep relaxation.

Can one control caution and wonder? Control, in this new way, does not involve ego. Rather it is a release of self into the flow. A "letting go," a dropping or melt down of self into the blend, melding, melting Grand Flow.

### Tuesday, November 9, 2021
### The Hatching of Newself

Corona and clotting smashed my old self-image. Transition and change are the new mode. I stand at the precipice of inner peace and wisdom. But I also ask, what happened to daring and wild? Have they been drained out of me? I'm, not sure.

I'd like to bring being daring and wild onto this precipice.

Inner peace, wisdom, daring and wild: A nice combination for my next life.

### Wednesday, November 10, 2021
### Continuing the Re-Entry Process

I woke up with the first headache I've had in years. It means I am angry. At what? I've given up being daring and wild. Do I want to find them in me again? I have given up videos, promoting and advertising, tours, concerts, and depth diving. However, happily a new goal has suddenly emerged: Folk dance sales. Aim for twenty people Monday night. Call dancers. Sell and promote.

Use my books, concerts, readings as advertising and promotion. Give them away free. All to promote Monday night folk dancing—as a start.

### Freshness Starts in the Land of Failure

I need a place to lose, a place to fail! I need a visit to the Land of Failure, where I can experiment, try new things, dream, hope, fall on my face, humiliate myself, make as many mistakes as I want, all with impunity, laugher, and love. I need my failures, along with my successes.

Freshness starts in the land of failure.

I can start failing today. Even this morning in my folk dance class. Approach it with the dynamic, Thomas Edison failure attitude. Wide open with wonder.

### Friday, November 12, 2021
### Gestation

Monastery life has ended. I'm gestating. My meditations, transitions, and new directions are taking hold.

New and different. The cells of my body are preparing to create a new body to fit my new mind-set.

Rest, sleep, and time are handmaidens of the gestation process.

There's no rushing. It takes as long as it takes.

# Redesigning My Brain

*Sunday, November 14, 2021*
*Work and Love*

Is my work the only thing that will get me out of the house? Force me to socialize and see people? Freud said work and love make the world go round. I love my work. Does it make mine go round?

To me, it equals business, being a social director, and people. It is my form of giving to others.

So art and study are incomplete without their finale of service—expressing of love for others. Which means I also love business!

If I love my business and my business expresses love, why do I resist it so much? Why am I humiliated by sales, promotion, and advertising? The inner, monkish artistic self is ever in conflict with the outer, service oriented, social-director, giving self.

Can this conflict ever be resolved?

I have somehow decided these dual aspects of my nature are in conflict. The separation, disunion, of art and business is *my decision*. Why have I kept them separate so long?

For protection. To protect the magnificent visions, glories and treasures of my imagination. The outer world threatens my inner one. Fear of criticism and humiliation was too great. I was never strong enough to fight back, to challenge the monsters. Instead, as a teenager I retreated into my violin practice room. As an adult I continued my retreat by entering the monastic, artistic world of my imagination. So lovely and relaxing.

Well, that was my old life. But now, after a year and a half of monkish Corona-life meditation, I have revised my attitudes. I want to return stronger, better, and different.

Can I now unite art and business, fuse the inner and outer, idealistic monk and material world, solo and inclusive, private practice and public performance, giving and taking, fantasy and skills, work and love?

The only way to return differently is with a different attitude. A united one. Dialectically opposite selves would have to synthesize into a new all-is-one.

This is a lovely dream. On one level, I have no choice. In order to take the next step forward, I have to unite them. But will I? If I do, it means returning with a vengeance, a rage that pushes me into war with my monsters, Mr. Maelstrom Concert and Mrs. Jagged Mountain Performance.

### Wednesday, November 17, 2021
### Stay in Being and Gestate

I'm reading *The Body Keeps The Score*, by Bessel Van Der Kolk. It's about trauma. Did I ever have a trauma? Somehow, I wish I did, so I can relate to this book. Being unable to play "Alhambra" or perform for so many years must have come from some sort of trauma. But I can't remember having one.

Perhaps I have redesigned my brain so the trauma has faded, been forgotten, even disappeared. Perhaps my chosen path of neuroplastic personal change through new thought patterns is working.

It feels like I'm sailing into a new land.

My so-called "trauma test" can be found in my ability to play hat piece. And each day playing it is easier and more beautiful. (I'm taking "Leyenda" along with it.) I'm accepting and believing my success and new confidence will continue.

This morning I have no desire for growth or self-improvement. I only want to stay in being and gestate in wholeness.

### Friday, November 19, 2021
### Risk: No Risk in Trading

I like risk. It wakes me up, alerts me. It also "relaxes" me by totally focusing my mind. Does this explain stock trading? Partly. In trading, over the long term, I usually lose money.  So I must ask: Is there really a risk in it? How can there be if, for me, loss has been certain?  True, I have *hope* that some day I will win.  But long term, over the months and years, I never do.  Why do it?

Well, if I give up trading, where will I *find* risk?

*Sunday, November 21, 2021*
*Normalizing the Gains*

Now I know why I ached all day yesterday, especially in my lower back and legs.  It was a juncture point, passage into the new life.  Old cells died, were being destroyed in order to make room for the new replacement cells needed for my upcoming new life.

Next step is to normalize my gains.

*Self-Improvement as a Good-in-Itself*

Why is self-improvement the best road for me to follow?  Because the constant challenge of self-improvement, of daily working, trying, rising, climbing higher on Jacob's ladder, stimulates, excites, and focuses me!  Without this, I slip into lack of energy, a directionless existence, a meaningless life.  However, I'm now in a new place.  Self-improvement is for internal, personal reasons.  My mental landscape has changed.  Yes, others will benefit. They do with any self-improvement.  But I have had a slow but cataclysmic mental shift.  Through many months of monastic training, aided by the Covid retreat, my thinking has reversed direction, moving from outward to inward.  Confidence through personal revelation has solidified. Now I know self-improvement is good. And I know why!  It is simply a good *for me*.

*Friday, November 26, 2021*

Guitar philosophy or message: The world is off-beat, which means it's upbeat.  Life's emphasis or accent is off-beat. Thus, think upbeat. Express this off-beat philosophy through guitar. And paradoxically, do this even when the music of your life is on the beat!

Such as in Sor's "Etude Number 12" in 3/4 time. Emphasize first beat. On the beat! The study emphasizes relentless, persistent, never give up. In "Alhambra" 3/4, emphasize/accent second and third beat. So much easier, right, and meaningful. In "Leyenda" 3/4, emphasize first beat. On the beat!

Heart-beat of the universe ringing out on the first note of each measure, driving and relentless, sounding out the fundamental meaning of the world.

### Self-Expression and Guitar

I am so lucky to play guitar! These classical pieces are my pieces. I express, press out, my moods through them now, at the very moment. When I do that, I submit to the healthy freedom of expression, the truth of here-and-now, its vitality, excitement, and dynamic of seizing the moment. I bow to *carpe diem*.

### Saturday, December 4, 2021
### Family Tradition

I'm quite surprised, and even a bit embarrassed, that these pages keep filling up with words like God, religion, and spiritual, so distant from my upbringing. In fact, they were never mentioned, even scorned. Religion was the opiate of the people. And talk of God? Forget it? No such thing as this illusion, phantom, ghost existed. Only for stupid people.

So here I am following and believing the exact opposite of what I was taught when I grew up. But is it really the opposite? I want to think not, because I'd like to belong to a good family tradition. But, truly, communism, with its shallow atheism, sucks. And that, unfortunately, was my family tradition. So I'm the ultimate rebel—quiet, smiling, and friendly, but rebel nevertheless.

Rebellion though, was also part of my family tradition. So maybe I do belong. In my family, artists and intellectuals were worshipped; they were the gods. And artists especially (along with some intellectuals) were rebels. And admired as such.

So as a rebellious artist, I belong to my family tradition, and my artistry can be admired as such. But never my anti-communist, pro-Trump, so-called "conservative" (once called "liberal") political views! Total anathema to my family and friends.

So I stand alone. I'm definitely out of the family and friends mainstream. No one in my family agrees with me. Friends: maybe one or two. But strangely, my position is not so bad. I know I'm right, at least for me. I'm just a bit quiet about it, especially in public, since I don't like being hit.

## Sunday, December 5, 2021
### The Wisdom of Walking

A beautiful sunny day today. I took a long a walk. In the beginning, my legs hurt. Quads especially very tight. Here are some random thoughts on pain, pleasure, power, and relaxation that came up en route.

Walks are about transforming pain into pleasure. Or, put another way, transforming pain into power! You can achieve it through deep relaxation. Pain hides power; power hides pain. Thus, pain is power; power is pain. Deep relaxation removes the pain cover, the power lid. In the process, it makes pain disappear.

So I suggest beginning each walk, or exercise, with a deep focus on relaxation. Even though sometimes you have to fake it to eventually feel it, deep relaxation is a skill that works.

## Friday, December 10, 2021
### I Need Romance

There's no romance in simple body and muscle questions. Evidently, I need a flight of imagination to inspire me. What is romance but a flight of imagination? What is imagination but eternity? The body is limited, but imagination is limitless. It can go anywhere! And anywhere is exactly where I want to go.

So I need to stay in touch with my imagination every day in order to motivate me to go anywhere and do anything. And this includes calligraphy and singing,

### Sunday, December 12, 2021
### Perfect "Alhambra"

I just played the perfect "Alhambra." Relaxed, slow, easy, my mind in a sublime state. And this after the beautiful discovery that Bach's "Gavotte en Rondeau" is based on a melody, a theme of only three notes! Same for his "Gavotte in D." Three notes, sprinkled around and hidden is so many unique ways. Simple and complicated at the same time.

Now I move on to a slow and focused "Leyenda."

When my focus flags, one of the ways I move away from the truth of the moment is by asking, "What's the purpose of my guitar practice?" And I give myself answers like: Give others pleasure, play for others, perform for them, give concerts, heal the world. All grand abstractions.

Due to fatigue, I enter the world of abstractions. Can anything be done about this? Is it even worth the bother? Perhaps becoming aware is enough, simply accepting fatigue as part of the human condition. The magic of self-awareness slices through many problems, softening their harshness, dropping the remnants into Land of Forgetfulness, and allowing you to move on.

### Relish the Focus

Learn to stop at the right time. What a mental skill that is! How to stop where focus ends and fatigue begins. And how to relish the focus!

### Love Conquers All: Language and Memory

Drop attempts to memorize foreign words. Rather, focus on love of their sounds, the feel of holding a letter in my mouth, the sensuality of pronouncing it. Do this, and memorizing words will happen naturally by itself.

But whether it works or not is beside the point.
Love is what counts.
Love the language.

### Wednesday, December 15, 2021

Where do you go after success?
To the next top!

But before you find the next mountain, you descend into the valley, there to recover, rest, and meditate—perhaps on the short-term pleasure of success. Then, after walking in the valley of emptiness, disappointment, and despair, you eventually come upon the next mountain. Once that climb begins, despair dissolves in challenge. The next peak comes into view.

# Run Wild on Freedom Road

*Thursday, December 16, 2021*
*Moving into Dance and Performance*

Yesterday I took videos of my Wednesday folk dance class and my latest choreographies.  First videos I've taken in almost two years, first since the advent of the Corona\virus disaster.

Strangely, after months of Covid attitude cleansing, I feel very different.  And now I know why.  I am moving into dance and performance. How cool is that! Cleansed and hopeful, my body aches, but in a new way.

*Friday, December 17, 2021*
*Miracle of Transformation*

Suddenly, I feel like I'm falling apart.  And I am.

Falling apart is so typical of mental changes. When my mind changes, my body changes with it. As old brain cells die, I feel it. This transformation continues as I flounder and fiddle, trying to find new directions, levels, and goals. Once I do, my disparate energies suddenly bind together, mobilize, and then, just as suddenly, all my aches and pains disappear!

*The Joys of Stock Trading*

When Covid started, I thought my folk dance and tour careers were over, and that I'd better find a new way of making a living.  I also thought it was my chance to give trading stocks a complete and thorough try, see how good I could be at it, since I could now devote all of my time to it. Maybe I could even make it my new profession!

So I spent almost the last two years trading stocks. The first year it was full time. The second year, as folk dance classes opened up a bit, I cut back some.

I first broke even but eventually ended up losing money. Very discouraging. So discouraging in fact, that I decided to give it up. This giving up has often taken place in the past, especially during losing periods. But I have always come back to it. This time the same thing happened. I gave up trading for a few days, but now I'm back.

What are the results of this up-and-down, back-and-forth, zig-zag trading adventure? Here they are: Stock trading is my great entertainment, distraction, and hobby. In a strange way, its up-and-down excitement and distraction also relax me.

It has no purpose beyond that.

### Saturday, December 18, 2021
### Embrace Depressions

Rather than deny depression, why not embrace it? Although it rarely brings joy, it often brings health. Depression is the black hole where comfort and misery meet.

Strangely, I often climb in after a success. Upon achieving a big goal, my direction and sense of meaning dissolve, and my ego falls into the abyss. Down, down, down, the descent feels endless. The fall itself is the depression.

However, once I hit the soft, muddy soil of Bottom, I begin sucking on the disgusting creatures I find there, imbibing their bitter juices, gobbling up their fertilizing nutrients. Soon my belly is full. Then, nourished with new energy and ideas, I begin my next climb. Not bad. And once I start, depression dissolves, seems to disappear. But it never really disappears. Rather, it is transformed into ascension.

### Excitement

Here's a great question: Are my present impediments and discouragements another type of excuse to avoid excitement? After all, this has been my psychological problem in the old neighborhood past. Am I bringing this old habit into my new neighborhood? In other words, now that I've succeeded in conquering my old demons, am I creating new ones to take their place? Moving forward, do I still want, or need, demons to challenge me so I can overcome them?

I'm leaning toward the idea it's just another excuse for me to hold back, restrain myself, limit freedom, not seize the moment, not dive into the here-and-now.

## Summation

I used to be afraid I'd have no money, couldn't play classical guitar, or perform a concert. Through the Covid period, those fears have evaporated. Can I live without fears? Probably not.

So I've replaced them with new ones: fears of frailty and death. Of course, they existed when I was younger. Only they were covered up by financial and performance fears.

Now, here they are. Whether old or new, though, the constant is fear. And, I do need realistic fears, yes. Unrealistic, anxiety fears, no. Were financial and performing fears real? Partly. Are frailty and death fears real? Partly.

*Most* fears are partly real. But due to monkey mind, they keep coming, appearing, never stopping as it jumps from one tree to another.

Seems that only "diving in" stops monkey mind. Focusing on the present alleviates fears by forgetting about them.

The answer is: Turn off your mind.

## The World of Faster

It's easier playing faster now because I'm beyond the dam. No walls are holding me back; the waters are flowing freely. Faster means looser, opening side, flowing, relaxed. It loosens muscles, opens them up, lengthens the fibers, lets them flow.

If it's easier playing the guitar faster, I wonder if it's also easier folk dancing faster. Fast dances, after all, loosen up the muscles.

When the dam opens, body, soul, and spirit are free to flow on Freedom Road.

### Monday, December 20, 2021

"Soleares" and "Gavotte en Rondeau": Playing them is so easy now. I've crossed the line, dizzy with confusion and happiness as I enter my new home.

There's no stopping the flow. Grateful am I.

Thank you for this blessing.

### Tuesday, December 21, 2021

Once again, fantastic and beautiful guitar playing. I'm in a new place.

Can I bring my blessings to others? Or is sharing automatic? Is sharing the very nature of a blessing? No effort from me is necessary. It automatically goes out. All is One. And higher vibrations, although they may come to visit me, are, by their very nature, simultaneously bestowed upon and shared by all.

### Wednesday, December 22, 2021
### Knowledge and/or Wisdom

What's the difference between knowledge and wisdom? Knowledge (or smartness): The more you know, the more complicated it gets. Knowledge divides.

Wisdom: The wiser you are, the simpler it gets: Wisdom unites. I'd like to play my guitar wisely and unite my audience. And simultaneously weld together all the disparate parts of my monkey mind.

### Friday, December 24, 2021
### Floating with Dinosaurs in a Tyrannobyte Universe

I have been practicing guitar for a concert that will never be. How strange is that? Maybe not so strange. No forced concert, or compulsion of any kind, is the essence of the new neighborhood I'm entering.

The idea of composing music came up. It seemed like a good one but soon fizzled out.

In fact, all my former ideas about wanting, needing direction, and having a purpose keep fizzling out. I'm ending up with no goal, purpose, or direction. I'm simply floating in space, wandering aimlessly here and there, light on purpose, causes, and goals. Light on everything. Just floating. Not bad. But not good either.

## Saturday, December 25, 2021
### Parables of Gustav

Gustav sat down to play his first piece: "The Magic of A Minor." "Ah, to improve and compose on the vine," he sighed.

"You mean On the Di-vine," his schizophrenic incubator added, placing one toe in the Atlas Ocean, the other in the Celestial Sea.

## Sunday, December 26, 2021
### Infinite Dissatisfaction/Eternal Motivation: The Forever Path

A combination of arrogance and fatigue makes me believe I stand on the highest rung. Intellectually, I know this cannot be true. But physically and emotionally, I'm exhausted. So I claim victory. That way I can take a break. After all, I've conquered "Alhambra." Now I'll embark on that much-needed vacation.

Well, I may need a rest. But that doesn't mean I've reached the end. There is no end. Infinity and eternity are endless. And that's where I am. I just hesitate to admit it. Breaks and stops along the way. But otherwise, no rest for the weary. Strangely, I like it that way!

Yes, the body will die. It will be painful and disorienting. But there's no escaping the ladder. Climbing is forever on the terrestrial plane; and perhaps other planes as well.

So as an Earth dweller, make the most of it. Can I go deeper? Of course. Could it be a goal? Of course. Is there a depth beyond death? Probably. But if there is, I seem to make any excuse to avoid it. And yet

I flourish best with a long-term goal. My present contentment and satisfaction are temporary resting places. Time to move on.

### Wednesday, December 29, 2021
### Grandiose

One of Irvin Yalom's characters in *Lying on the Couch* observes that "grandiosity need not be abandoned. It's the ego's natural way of staving off the limitations, the dreariness and despair of everyday life."

I like it. So keep practicing guitar. . .for that concert in the sky. Can limitless and limited be united? Can you live in two worlds at once? Yes. It's called remembering who you are.

### Friday, December 31, 2021
### Sickness

I've had a terrible cold the past few days. I've stopped all physical activities. Luckily, all work is on vacation as well.

What is the purpose of getting sick? Sickness is a cleansing. When I am clean, clarified, the sickness will have served its purpose, and I will be cured. What has been cleaned out? Old attitudes. When my new attitude is firmly in place, I will get better.

I'll play with confidence and give a powerful "Alhambra" performance!

So, until I can do this, I'll remain clogged up, unclear, unclean, and ill. But most important, performing the "Alhambra" before others terrifies me! That is the real reason I'm sick and continue to be sick.

Although terror is a ghost I've invented, nevertheless, I have to jump through the haunted mist, the cloud over the abyss. Someday hopefully, I'll land in a safe place.

Yes, what stupidity to let others judge me. But I do. What's the matter with me? Where did my judgement and courage go? Am I crazy to leave who and what I am in the clapping hands of others? Madly off my rocker. Best to send this rocking chair hurtling down into the abyss.

Why did I invent the ghost in the first place? Not to bow *to* the judgement of others, but to free myself *from* the judgement of others! Maybe I've been misinterpreting this ghost. Maybe it means something else. What is lying in the abyss under the mist, cloud, and veil that the ghost has created?

Could it simply be self-confidence and power? I can't *wait* for an audience to crown me king. I can't put that decision in *their* hands. I have to crown *myself* king. And do it with the help of God, or whoever He or She may be.

Is that hubris? Maybe. But I could use some grandiosity along with a few oversized, overabundant dreams. These, along with some mischievous, playful, malevolent help from Hermes, will, I'm sure, help me succeed.

Can I use a polytheistic god in my climb out of the gutter? What will HaShem say? Maybe nothing. Maybe He agrees. His wife says, use whatever works.

# New Neighborhood

### Leyenda Barre

Mischievous equals rebellious, dissident. Look into the foundational guitar structures. Example: "Leyenda" barre: Blow it up, destroy, re-examine, start over. Ask and explore new questions. Can my left pinky, through deep relaxation and focus, be stretched further during the barre passages?

I'm choosing "barre." Why? Its double R is thicker, needs more power and strength to pronounce. Same with barre: the word needs more power and strength to press and play. Even though power and strength can be found through relaxation.

### Sunday, January 2, 2022

Business people take risks in the real world. Are there risks in a mon-astery? Maybe. But I don't know what they are.

### Standing Up To Hysteria

Standing up to hysteria is part of the new neighborhood. Should I speak out against it?

Probably not, since hysterics don't listen. On the other hand, even-tually maybe they will. In any case, the best approach is stand firm for reason.

Speaking out is good even though it *seems* no one is listening. Ac-tually, you never know who is listening, including the hysteric. And speaking out is good for you. It's good practice. You become familiar with the feeling of total rejection. When you do, you can stand alone more easily, with more confidence.

### Going Slow

Dealing with the trauma of going slow is my gateway into the new neighborhood. It's also the key to creativity in my classical guitar playing. And my personal slow trauma is found in my index finger, and thumb hypothenar muscles. (Also speaking slowly in public.)

Going slow, loving slow, is my key. Daily practice is the next step.

### Agile Fighting Power

When I am threatened, my first reaction is retreat. I become quiet and tighten internally as I withdraw. Silently churning, I try figuring out how to deal with my fear and anger, until I know what to do next. Could I learn to withdraw into a place of relaxation, looseness, and agile fighting power?

### Tuesday, January 4, 2022
### Impressing Others: A Source of Motivation

Got an email from Hope Player. "I'm so impressed by your line-up of tours," she said. How's that for a source of motivation! My source of motivation is to impress others! It's so base, crass, and egotistic, but it may work! And I sure need motivation!

Maybe it has been right all along. After all, impressing others is simply another way of saying I'm making them happy. And making others happy is a total blessing for both of us. So impressing others may well be the right way to go; it might put the best bounce in my spring. Being a total egotist, I would never admit this. But now I will. It's risky, and frightening. But fear is a big motivator.

### Wednesday, January 5, 2022
### I Like Speed! A Day of Fasting

Now that I can do it, I like speed! Guitar days of brilliant sunshine. I'm fasting today; my diet is speed. Watch "Alhambra" roll!

And from there, my Sor "Etude Number 12," "Bach Bourree in Bm," even "Gavotte en Rondeau." Roaring out at breath-taking speeds. Faster and faster. A giant train on the move. Even "Leyenda" teeters on the brink. Now it falls! Ah, rolling down the track at exuberant speeds! Lightning on the frets. Ah, it is glorious, exiting, exuberant, exhilarating!

### Thursday, January 6, 2022
### Problems

Yesterday's problems are not today's problem. Most of them get solved, or are in the process of getting solved, when I write about them. Plus you can never go backward, only forward. I solve my problems! I don't have to worry about forgetting my solutions.

Yet most of my problems keep returning. Are they the same ones? No. They may look the same, but they are different. They have matured, changed, been transformed, and now present themselves as next-level problems. So although the sun may rise every day and always looks the same, every day it is totally different. Very optimistic.

### Saturday, January 8, 2022
### Love and Joy: New Neighborhood Tools

Love feels like a melting into the Magnificence. Joy feels like excitement, a bubbling-up, dramatic. They are different feelings but forms of the same connection. Art expresses them. Love and joy are great healers, but as higher vibrations they are harder to see. When (and if) I see them, they become powerful positive motivators. I need to learn their secrets.

I'm putting Love and Joy in my left-hand "Alhambra" barre muscles. "Leyenda," too. While I'm at it, I'll send hot currents of Love into my stiff left shoulder.

The battle between fear and love begins again. It's taking place in my left-shoulder "Bach Gavotte in D" muscles. Warm up by sending currents of hot love into them. Stiff muscles are "cold with fear" and must be warmed with love so they can thaw, soften, and begin to flow. The battle between Love and Fear takes place on the battlefield of Stiff Muscles. Fibers cramp and hurt during the fight. They tighten periodically and must be taken off the battlefield. But after rest and relaxation, they heal and can fight again.

## Monday, January 10, 2022

Fabulous morning at the gym! I came out light, airy, and happy as a feather.

Part of being tough and resilient is accepting a great day!

## Tuesday, January 11, 2022
## Guitar Lips

The most courageous concert I could give would be to feel each string before I pluck it, and listen to the tone of each note. This means playing guitar so so so slowly.

How do I imagine the audience reaction? "Boring! Boring!" they scream. Or politely, they think, When will this fucker end? I paid all this money, and look what I'm getting? A big nothing! That's what I hear them saying—first to themselves, then to others around them. A complete disaster.

And yet, in this imagined concert, I'd courageously keep playing. I'd feel each string before I plucked it, and listen to each note after I played it. Slow, slow, slow. Tone is the word. So meditative. Tempo is beside the point. Sure, I may soon play faster and move easily into a fluid, up-beat tempo. But again, maybe not. It depends on how I feel. The courage part is daring to give the concert, forget obligation to the audience, and focusing on how I feel.

Is this possible? A good thing to do? After all, one doesn't "take" a concert, one "gives" it. And focusing on my feelings means taking the time from the audience, forcing them to sit there while I do what I want. Somehow it feels "selfish." That's because it *is* selfish. Can one give a selfish concert? Can I put myself first? I don't think so. When I stand before an audience, it is my natural instinct to please them.

I'd love to focus only on my slow, tone-creating self. But that would

182 / JIM GOLD

not be a concert.

What to do? I don't know. Maybe never give a concert again. Play only for my alter ego. But even in this scenario, before I wow them with fluidity, tone, and speed, I still have to bore them with slow plucking, majestic sound, and the strong tone emanating from my guitar lips.

I hate to say it, but the above writing is just bullshit. Truth is, I'm just finding new excuses to avoid giving a concert. I'm taking the coward's way out. First step is to admit it. Do I have the right to be a coward? Yes. Do I want to be?

Have Faith
Muse is spirit. Spirit is muse.
The spirit muse floats in and out.
It's fickle that way. What to do?
Persevere. Perseverance counts.
Stick with it no matter what.
Go through the motions,
Do it anyway, even without spirit;
Have faith:
The bird will fly again.

### Happy Fingers

4:40 p.m. Afternoon "Alhambra": My fingers are so happy to play In fact, I'm thinking that they've never been this happy! Such unabated, whole-hearted, and total happiness. No pressure, no place to go, no nothing. Just flowing, relaxed, sinking, I dive into the finger moment!

### Eternal Life

I am looking for God and Eternal Life. That's what my journal is all about. Bringing my vision of Him to the world.

Perhaps that is my job. . .through many lifetimes.

## Wednesday, January 19, 2022
## Awe-and-Wonder Guy

Awe and wonder win the day. Do I deserve them? Do I deserve the good thoughts I'm thinking, the good things that are happening to me?

Deserve? I've never used this word before. Am I grateful?

Or am I entitled? Perhaps a bit of both. Entitlement has fear behind it. The word is usually applied to government. If given by government, it can be taken away by government. Thus, entitlements are not truly mine. If I am merely entitled to the good things I'm thinking, doing, and getting, I could lose them. Of course, on a larger level, nothing I think, do, or get is really mine. It can all can be taken away by fate and its Higher Powers.

"Gratitude" is a better word for receiving these gifts. "Thank you, Lord, for the good thoughts I am thinking. Thank you for the quiet, peaceful, fruitful, creative, fulfilling life I am living." In reality, long term, I don't own a thing. Even my mind and feelings are on loan. But I do have a choice of attitude. And the one I choose is awe and wonder.

## End of Corona

Strange, but suddenly I don't mind wearing masks. It started when the gym re-instituted mask wearing with the advent of the Omicron virus. I didn't mind it. In fact, wearing one felt familiar, comfortable, even comforting. Now I could hide myself once again behind a mask, in my cocoon of self.

Is there some sadness in this "enjoyment and acceptance?" I sense that this corona period, along with its mask wearing, social distancing, strange rituals, and all its other craziness will eventually be coming to a close.

I feel the ending in the air. This wild, unhinged, frightening, enraging, isolating period has been rich in challenges and personal changes. I've grown and developed in surprising new ways. And strangely, part of me will miss it.

*Friday, January 21, 2022*
*Imagination: Meeting Big Me*

Is it my imagination? Or is it the Universal Imagination filtered through the small imagination me? I lean toward the latter. To reach this peak, little me needs expansion to Big Me. When this enlightened state is realized, then playing guitar "alone" in my living room reaches All. because there is no such thing as alone.

*Monday, January 24, 2022*
*Reach High*

Glory is good. But ecstasy is best! No halfway measures here. Reach high. Go straight to the Big Guy.

*The Vibrational Truth*

My vibrations reach everyone in this world, whether I like it or not. That's the vibrational truth, So, whether I like it or not, am aware of it or not, my thoughts affect the world. What an awesome truth. Even in the privacy of my room, alone on a mountain, sitting in a cave miles from others, what I think matters! There is no escape. We are all One Vibration, scattered in all directions, but rolled into One.

What does this mean personally? During my yoga practice, when I maintain a shoulder stand, am I healing the necks of the world? Of course. And this happens whether I think it or not. But consciously emission is more powerful. When I focus on transmitting the healing, it helps others and myself even more.

The vibrational connection is strengthened by ecstasy. So for example, during yoga practice, as you focus on your stretch, imagine sending the vibrations to everyone else in the world. A hamstring stretch stretches all the hamstrings in the world; the blood rushing to the head in a headstand brings blood to the brains of others as far away as Africa, the moon, and Mars; it even creates new brain cells with healthier thoughts. Try it with my folk dances. Transmit the grapevine, two-step, hora, and more to the world.

So whether I believe it or not, what I do and think affects others.

### Tuesday, January 25, 2022
### First Concert on Mars

Plan a fantasy concert on Mars, with fantasy date, place, time, location, audience, etc. Funny, off-beat, off-the-wall, wild, crazy. (I'm rolling down the lawn laughing already!)  No audience, empty concert hall, no pressure except from the air around me.  First performance scheduled for flight to Mars.

Concert performance name: Looking Over the Abyss

Location: Edge of Hellas Basin crater (twice the size of Alaska, so lots of space for the non-existent audience.

Parking in local garages.

The program:  Concert free for *Zany* fans! What a bargain and deal! Group visits Mars to attend the first *Zany* concert.

### Saturday, January 29, 2022
### Light

Light comes before fast.  The invisible creates the visible.  Thoughts create the world. Practice light.  The lighter, the more imaginative, and with imagination you can go anywhere! Fast is concrete, and of the material world.  The combo of light and fast is dynamite!  Practice light, and fast will emerge by itself as a by-product.

### Sunday, January 30, 2022
### Faith and Confidence

Faith and confidence are the new neighborhood, the higher vibrations.  I am never alone. When I play guitar in my living room, the notes float across the universe reaching all.

The next challenge is to constantly remember this.

### Redefining Retirement as Victory

This is all about retiring. In the past, the idea of me "retiring" was so negative. It meant defeat and shame. Here I am a hero to myself for creating, sustaining, and, most important, making a living from my own artistic business. And this always in the face of incredible odds. Yes, I did it both as a guitarist in the concert business and as a folk dance teacher the folk dance and tour business.

I did them both for many years.

But now I have the problem of any winner. What do I do post-victory? How do I give up my past fields of glory and move on? What is the next level, the next stage? If any? Well, there is always a next stage. I just haven't figured out what it is yet.

But no question the old stage has served its purpose, fulfilled its mission. To remain on this formerly rich and hallowed ground means no moving on. And if I try to stay in it, it would soon turn foul and unclean. Ultimately, I would be rotting in place. Rotting is not for me. Even retirement is better than rotting. And the retirement vacuum, like any vacuum, will soon be filled.

So, first face and deal with all my old feelings of defeat, disgust, and shame over "retirement." Then redefine retirement as victory, winning, achieving, fulfilling my goals. Time to move on, find new goals, new mountains to climb.

### Saturday, February 5, 2022
### The Entertainment Business

I'm in the entertainment business.

The etymology of entertain is "to stretch or hold between." Studying languages is my form of entertainment. So is playing guitar. Life itself may simply be about entertaining yourself. What about learning and self-improvement? Isn't one put on Earth to learn things? Maybe they're all part of the entertainment process. When you entertain yourself, you learn something. And vice versa. So I am in the entertainment business.

### Is Seven the Magic Number?

Is there an optimum number of times to repeat an exercise? Rick says three is enough to get its maximum benefit. But now I'm wondering: How about seven? What happens when I repeat an exercise seven times? (Or even more?) Vladimir Horowitz repeated piano passages over a hundred times. And in one practice session! But let's start with seven.

# Return

# Return

*Thursday, February 10, 2022*
*Voyage of Mental Transformation*

Nothing has changed except my priorities, attitude, and self-defini-tion. But perhaps that is all that can ever change—and those changes are everything. New seeds sprout a new tree.

A new chapter begins. I even thought about finding others, training them to handle and help with the details, developing a JGI staff with a booker (quasi-sales person "secretary"), a designer, and folk tour dance guides. And some possible names for a new JGI tour branch of Bulgaria tours led by George Vishegonov: Golden Journeys, Sports Journeys, Co-rona (Virus) Tours, Outdoor (Sports) Adventure Journeys in Bulgaria, (Sports) Adventures in Bulgaria.

Slowly the plan is being revealed. I am the instrument.

*Sunday, February 13, 2022*
*Spring*

I have a big empty space in my heart. Part of it because we have lost Dick Wedeen, Janet is in hospice, and Hal is in the hospital. And on top of this, I have lost my guitar practice and stock trading distractions. A vast emptiness lies before me. I have nothing to do, nothing important with which to occupy myself. Is this empty feeling a prelude to writing?

*Sunday, February 20, 2022*
*Enjoy Business*

Last night strange words popped into my head: "Enjoy business." I've never said, or even considered, this before. Business, along with sales, was always something I had to do, forced to make a living so I could be "free" to be and become an artist (something I truly enjoyed).

But the possibility of enjoying business, marketing, sales, along with all business bookkeeping details, rose easily and naturally in my mind. Imagine! Where will this lead?

### "Retirement"

Second day of stunned and shocked. But the shock waves are lessening. I've fallen off the cliff. The bottom has fallen out. I'm facing the dreaded "retirement" word.

Disappointing others comes first. By retiring, I'm abandoning them completely.

This feels like guilt. But I don't believe in guilt. I only believe in fear. Am I disguising fear by feeling guilty? Probably. What am I afraid of? Loss. I'll miss all the people, my customers, contacts, and friends; I'll miss dealing and playing with them. I'll miss their smiles, camaraderie, complaints, conversations, all the actions, play, and adventures we had together. Yes, I feel loss, sadness, mourning, emptiness, falling off a cliff into the abyss of nothingness, purposelessness, and meaninglessness.

Sounds like fear to me. That's because it is fear. Fear that I'll be forgotten, become nothing, turn into a cipher, a meaningless dot in the universe. Does guilt also camouflage sadness? Yes.

Nice to know. This morning my wife said something so beautiful: "As the years go by, I love you more and more." And vice versa. Maybe retirement is liberation.

## ABOUT THE AUTHOR

Jim Gold likes to travel in many directions. He's a folk dance teacher, choreographer, musician, writer, and tour organizer. His novels, stories, journals, and choreography books chronicle his varied life. His classical guitar and folk song one-man show has appeared on TV, and in schools and universities across the U.S.A.

*Visit him at: www.jimgold.com.*

www.ingramcontent.com/pod-product-compliance
Lightning Source LLC
Chambersburg PA
CBHW020842260626
47169CB00003B/1101